LADY GAGA

Strange and Beautiful

The Fabulous Style of Lady Gaga

LADY GAGA

Strange and Beautiful

The Fabulous Style of Lady Gaga

Laura Coulman

Plexus, London

CONTENTS

INTRODUCTION
THE GOLDEN AGE OF GAGA

'I don't care what people **think about me . . .** I care what they think about themselves.'

In the beginning was the word . . . and the word? Naturally, it was Gaga. 'We are nothing without our image. Without our projection. Without the spiritual hologram of who we perceive ourselves to be, or to become, in the future,' she writes on the very first page of her hallowed 'Book of Gaga' – a mystery gift slipped into 10,000 Super Deluxe copies of her album, *The Fame Monster*. Spelled out in stark black letters, it's more than just another empty slogan; it's the passionate creed that defines Gaga's very existence, and the secret of how she transformed herself from timid Catholic schoolgirl into the most mesmerising show-woman on the planet.

Lady G's own personal biographer tells us that, 'When Lady Gaga was a little girl, she would sing along on her mini plastic tape recorder to Michael Jackson and Cyndi Lauper hits and get twirled in the air in daddy's arms to the sounds of the Rolling Stones and the Beatles . . . no wonder that [she] turned into the exhibitionist, multi-talented singer-songwriter [. . .] that she is today.' But the true story of Gaga's rise to the top is hardly so straightforward – drenched in stage blood and mascara tears, with many a moment of self-doubt along the way. A supremely gifted young musician, Stefani Germanotta had mastered the keys and penned her first piano ballad before she turned fourteen. Yet, her astounding natural talent didn't always shine through.

Only twenty kids in the world would have been lucky enough to gain early admission into Tisch, New York's most prestigious school of the arts. Seventeen-year-old Gaga was one of the chosen few. Yet she threw the opportunity away after just a few semesters. 'Once you learn how to think about art, you can teach yourself,' she shrugs. Clearly, the pop princess in-waiting had gotten 'frustrated'. Her decision was as follows: 'Fuck it! I will do whatever I want to do.' But what next? The alternative was anything but glamorous. Gaga remembers, 'I left my entire family, got the cheapest apartment I could find and ate shit until somebody would listen.'

Little did she suspect how long she'd have to wait, and while writing hits for the likes of Britney Spears (remember a track called 'Quicksand'? Those electrifying piano hooks came courtesy of the artist formerly known as Stefani) and New Kids On The Block was enough to pay the rent, her work as a faceless songwriter can hardly have been sufficient to satisfy Gaga's obsessive craving for artistry. Despite her admiration for the talented Ms Spears – 'I gotta say,' admits Gaga, '"Slave 4 U" was a moment for everyone. When that bitch came out with the slammin' body, we were all like, "We can't hate on you"' – it's always been Gaga's firm belief that: 'The last thing a young woman needs is another picture of a sexy pop star writhing in the sand, covered in grease, touching herself.'

As it happens, the Lady's own bedroom wall was decorated less conventionally. A record by Mrs John Lennon – the wonderfully wacky performance artist, Yoko Ono – was the last thing Gaga saw before closing her eyes each night. 'I'm not going to make a guy drool the way a Britney video does,' Gaga admits, but who's to say she'd even want to? A uniquely spellbinding performer, Gaga has been gifted with a charisma that's all her own. And her days in the shadows – watching silently in the wings while some other songstress took centre stage – were already numbered. 'I have always been an artist,' insists Gaga, her poker face deadly straight. 'And I've always been famous – you just didn't know it yet.'

Eventually the world would catch up. But it would take something more than raw musical talent to make Stefani's dreams come true. In today's MTV-obsessed society, what you see is at least as important as what you hear. She may have been praying for someone who would 'listen'; but what it really took for this focused young 'girl guidette' was someone prepared to take a second *look*.

'The last thing a young woman needs is another picture of a sexy pop star.'

Previous page: Crystal vision: all smoking shades and platinum bangs, Gaga recreates the cover of The Fame, *live onstage at 2008's Jingle Ball. Opposite: Gaga stacks her shimmering shoulders to the roof for one stellar performance at the Nokia Theatre, December 2009.*

'I'VE ALWAYS BEEN FAMOUS — YOU JUST DIDN'T KNOW IT YET.'

Just ask Rob Fusari, the 38-year-old mogul who ended up producing and co-writing Gaga's early hits. These days, Gaga's a girl who appreciates better than anyone that 'fashion and music go hand-in-hand – and they always should. It's the artist's job to create imagery that matches the music . . . they're intertwined'. But back when she was starting out, it took her older songwriting partner and on-off boyfriend to point this out. Fusari can still remember a time before Stefani – and the world – went Gaga. 'A couple of times, she came to the studio in sweatpants and I said, "Really, Stef? What if I had Clive Davis in here today? I should call the session right now. Prince doesn't pick up ice cream at the seven-eleven looking like Chris Rock. You're an artist now. You can't turn this on and off."'

Since Gaga first exploded onto the global scene, she's been papped in a dizzying array of deliciously different ensembles – from rainbow bubbles to ruby-red meat – but a sloppy tracksuit has certainly never been one of them. Having hungrily devoured video after video by her own personal gods of performance art – David Bowie, Grace Jones, Marilyn Manson and Freddie Mercury are the hallowed names recited by Gaga in interviews – it seems that Gaga has finally learned her lesson. 'Listen, I promise you, I don't wear slobby clothes,' the Lady protested on *Friday Night with Jonathan Ross*. 'I look impossibly fresh when I fall out of bed, but I would say this . . . that I would rather die than have my fans not see me in a pair of high heels!'

In Gaga's fashion wonderland, the symbolic

> **'Listen, I promise you, I don't wear slobby clothes . . . I would rather die than have my fans not see me in a pair of high heels!'**

power of spangled heels and glitzy designer creations is impossible to overstate. 'We are nothing without our image,' wrote Lady G, but she was almost certainly thinking of herself. Even if you're not familiar with Gaga's instantly irresistible hit songs, then you'll surely recognise her signature look – the platinum locks flowing out from beneath a little red riding hood; her coat of many Kermits; the cherry-red PVC doll who shook Her Royal Highness Queen Elizabeth by the hand. Such is Gaga's fondness for *The Wizard of Oz* that she's unleashed an electrified, horror-tinged version of her own on the world in the form of her Monster Ball tour. And, just as Dorothy – a plucky young heroine who manages to look good even in the midst of a tornado – clings to her ruby slippers as magical protection from the Wicked Witch of the West, so Gaga wraps herself in impenetrable layers of blood-stained lace, glitter bone and orbiting rings of steel. A masked mistress of disguise, veiled in smoke and lace and feathers, she always looks as though she's headed for a midnight 'carnival in Venice' – as Madonna herself once commented.

Meanwhile, the girl behind the superstar avatar remains tantalisingly out of reach. Whatever Stefani's truly feeling behind her picture-perfect poker face is anyone's guess. Surrounded by an aura of electrifying mystique so real you want to reach out and touch it (mesmerised DJ Scott Mills went so far as to try backstage at the 2009 Brit Awards), these days Gaga's persona is always 'on' – and her darling little monsters wouldn't have it any other way.

Neither, it seems, would the haters – as embodied by the tabloid press. 'They've tried everything,' Gaga told *Rolling Stone* in 2010,

Opposite: Bow down: Gaga graces Germany's Dome 49, working this cute glossy gown like a PVC princess, February 2009.

'when they start saying that you have extra appendages [with rumours that Gaga is a hermaphrodite] you have to assume that they're unable to destroy you. I've got scratch marks all over my arms, and they say I'm a heroin addict. It's from my costumes. When I pass out onstage, they say that I'm burning out, when I have my own a) personal health issues, and b) it's hot up there and I'm busting my ass every night.'

Either way, bad press is a thing undreamt of in Gaga's philosophy. 'I'd rather people love me or hate me than have no opinion of me,' she states simply. 'Indifference is scary.' But thanks to the Haus of Gaga – her team of tirelessly creative young designers who work day and night to make Gaga's deepest dreams prêt-à-porter – there's little danger that Gaga's weird and wonderful fashion creations will ever meet with this reaction. Love her or loathe her, Gaga's the one-woman phenomenon you simply can't ignore.

Whether she's catching a plane wearing nothing but her bra and PVC panties or attending her sister's graduation from convent school in the guise of a thrilling, frilly bee-keeper, Gaga's kooky fashion sense can always be counted upon. In the mind of this fearless young fashionista all the world's a catwalk – and this alone makes for some dangerously addictive observation. When a bemused newsreader at CNN asked Gaga, 'How do you even know what to wear?' she was surely speaking for an entire generation. In terms of gaga fashion, Lady G is raising the bar to outrageous new heights. 'Every time I get on the stage,' babbled Gaga excitedly, 'I do something different. I want people to think, "Every time I have this bitch nailed down, she does something different."' But if the appeal of the 'Gaga show' rests solely on the singer's ability to outdo herself with each and every outlandish new outfit, then the Monster Ball could soon be over.

As journalist Kira Cochrane once warned, 'Shock will eat itself.' At the 2010 Video Music Awards, Gaga unveiled her most controversial costume yet. Sewn from the very finest cuts of beef – fresh from designer Franc Fernandez's family butcher – her super-rare dress still failed to impress. Apparently, Cochrane and her contemporaries require their steak flame-grilled or not at all. 'The meat dress attracted attention at a time when Gaga's very unpredictability had begun to seem predictable, when her constant innovation had threatened to drag,' writes a cranky Cochrane. 'Some of the writers and commentators I spoke to for this piece – many of whom love her – professed that they'd nevertheless become slightly weary of the newness, of the fact that every day Gaga would wear something, say something, do something that seemed primed to provoke a blog, an article, a comment.'

Yet anyone who believes this has grossly misunderstood what Gaga is all about. Ironically enough, the Lady herself had this to say: 'I don't consider my own clothing to be outrageous . . . The truth is that people just don't have the same references that I do. To me it's very beautiful and it's art.' Step inside Gaga's spaceship-sized wardrobe and you'll realise her fashion choices run deeper than many critics could ever believe. To dismiss the Lady as an attention-craving diva, specialising in shock without substance, is to miss the artistry behind many of her haute-couture creations. Crafted by some of the most illustrious names in fashion

Opposite: Read my lips: pieced together from the shattered remains of a disco ball, Gaga brings the Venetian carnival to Berlin with her own crazed take on an Italian classic, July 2009.

'I don't consider my own clothing to be outrageous . . . To me it's very beautiful and it's art.'

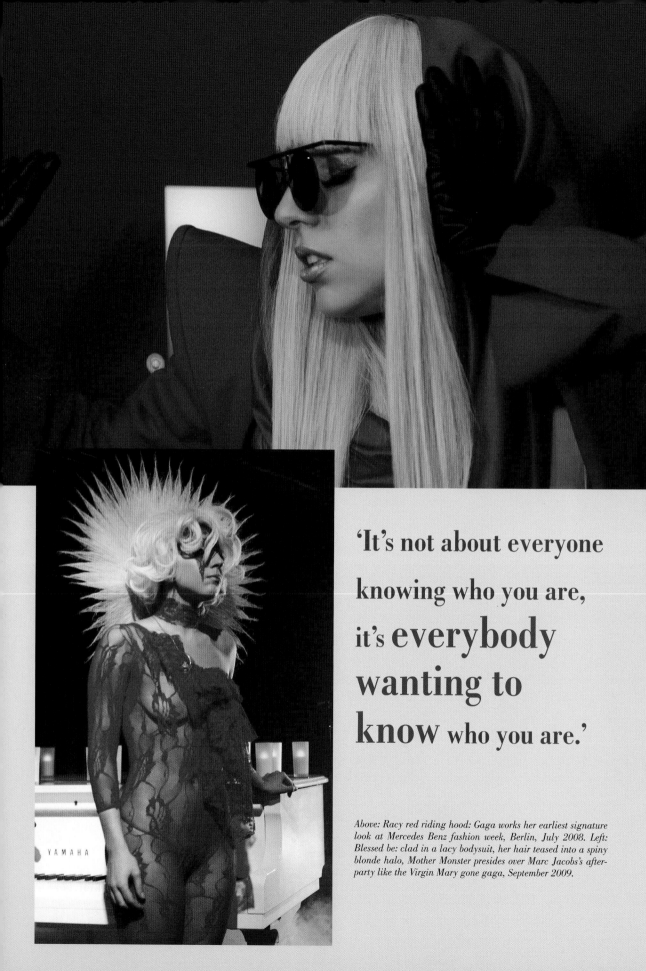

'It's not about everyone knowing who you are, it's **everybody wanting to know** who you are.'

Above: Racy red riding hood: Gaga works her earliest signature look at Mercedes Benz fashion week, Berlin, July 2008. Left: Blessed be: clad in a lacy bodysuit, her hair teased into a spiny blonde halo, Mother Monster presides over Marc Jacobs's after-party like the Virgin Mary gone gaga, September 2009.

– from Alexander McQueen to Philip Treacy – Gaga's outfits are so much more than vapid one-night wonders. Well worthy of exhibition at Paris's Chappe Gallery – where Gaga's fabulous frocks are currently attracting little monsters from all corners of the globe – each of her most compelling garments represents a lovingly crafted, achingly original work of wearable art. And more besides . . .

Take a second look at the darkened beauties showcased within these pages and you'll realise the truth of Gaga's claim that music and fashion are impossibly, inseparably 'intertwined'. Like two sides of the same dazzling coin, Gaga's garments are the concrete embodiment of her most heartfelt lyrics. If ever there was a Lady who wore her heart on her sleeve for all to see, then it's Gaga. Never content just to sing it, Mother Monster showed the world what it was to grow up 'Beautiful, Dirty, Rich' – dressing as a lacy red riding hood who'd most definitely strayed from the path. All flowing blonde extensions and no pants, she's never forgotten her hooded leotard combo. 'You know, I wanted to wear something that really represented my style so it's a special look for me,' recalls Gaga.

But as the lyrics took a turn for the darker, so did Gaga's sense of style. Listen closely to the mournful melodies of Gaga's wound-down tango 'Alejandro' and you'll realise that this is a tale of Latin love gone sadly wrong. More star-crossed than starry-eyed, the song is a bitter antidote to 'Fernando', the sunniest of all ABBA's classic love songs. Though the blogosphere may have mocked – 'Why is Lady Gaga dressed like a damn corpse?' tweeted one irate blogger. 'Hell, she could even depress the devil' – there was nothing fake about Gaga's morose new look.

Whereas David Bowie – Stefani's notoriously fickle idol – was content to hide behind his own 'perfect plastic rock star' Ziggy Stardust for just a few short years before sentencing him to death, Gaga is more than just 'protection' for Stefani – or so the Lady claims. 'It's just an expression of my artistry – which is fully what I am . . . when you decide to marry yourself to something you have to let go of what comes before it and you have to mourn it like a death. So . . . that's the obsession with death and darkness and fear and the change in the music – the industrial, the dance side, the gothic side – that's where that comes from. I am mourning, so it's not a persona – it's just who I've become. And when you become something that is your destiny, you have to let the rest go.'

Yet Gaga's poker face – unreadable as ever – belies her every word. 'People say Lady Gaga is a lie and they are right. I am a lie,' she told *Rolling Stone* weeks later. 'Every day I kill to make it true.' But with Mother Monster's gift for spellbinding performance, who cares if it's just another beautiful lie?

'It's not about everyone knowing who you are,' she whispers, a wicked twinkle in her eye. 'It's everybody *wanting* to know who you are.' And, for as long as she can keep on poker-facing, our fascination with this slippery fashion chameleon will never die. 'I'm just trying to change the world, one sequin at a time,' the Lady herself once wrote. Providing a tantalising glimpse at each of Gaga's favourite fashion fixations, this book will show how she's 'killing every day' to make it true. Prepare to take a step through the looking glass and into a contrary wonderland where all you'll see is Gaga . . .

'I'm just trying to change the world, one sequin at a time.'

THROUGH THE LOOKING GLASS

'You know, I don't really ever compare myself to other people and I don't even measure myself in terms of anyone but myself . . . I'm on a journey with myself.'

'We were *Born This Way*, baby!' snarled a leather-clad Gaga at MTV's 2010 Video Music Awards. A glinting silver 'moon man' in her grasp (one of the eight trophies she scored that evening) and a sea of adoring little monsters at her feet – four-inch killer heels to be precise – she was the undisputed queen of the night. And yet, something about Mother Monster's fierce new album title still rings false. . .

'Tonight, little monsters, we are the cool kids at the party!' Gaga proudly proclaimed, with a smile as dazzling as the diamanté jewels at her throat. But it wasn't always this way. Once upon a time, Lady Gaga was *baby* Gaga – a self-conscious Catholic schoolgirl who kept her dreams of dressing like Boy George to herself. This same mousy-haired 'theatre chick' has since emerged as pop's most fearless fashionista, but it is hardly the way she was born.

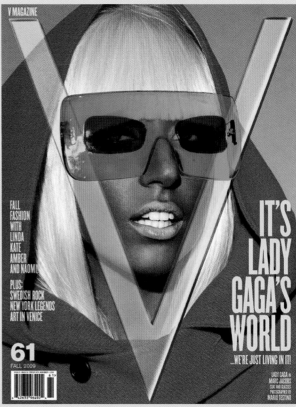

Stefani Joanne Angelina Germanotta was the name given to Gaga at birth. Yet, 24 years on, the artist formerly known as 'Stefani' retains not even this much of her younger self. Striding across the stage to collect her VMA, a crown of wicked black spines set upon her golden locks, you'd be forgiven for mistaking the New Yorker for the Statue of Liberty made flesh, and swiftly recruited as the token female member of Mötley Crüe. The vampy, voluminous jet creation she wore – sculpted to sadomasochistic perfection – came courtesy of none other than design legend Giorgio Armani. 'This outfit's too heavy to walk in. I apologise if I'm a little slow this evening,' quipped Gaga, dubbing the gothic wonder, 'fashion road kill'.

The metamorphosis of Stefani Germanotta is a fascinating process indeed. Simone de Beauvoir, French godmother of feminism, famously commented, 'One is not born a woman, one becomes one,' referring to all that impressionable young girls learn from observing older female role models. So, how exactly does one become the chameleonic Lady Gaga? Whatever she's made of beneath myriad layers of rainbow bubble and blood-stained lace, shattered disco ball and candy-bone confection, Muppet-soft fuzz and slickest, sickest PVC, it's certainly something more complicated than sugar and spice and all things nice.

An inspiration to millions (at the time of writing, 'Lady Gaga' is the single most popular Halloween costume on the planet), Gaga looks to the cherished icons of her own adolescence for inspiration. 'Fashion is so deep in my blood that I could just cry just sitting here talking to you about it,' she gushed. And given her pedigree, the star's intense passion seems entirely understandable.

Gaga was raised in the centre of one of the world's fashion capitals, New York City. Her former high school, the Convent of the Sacred Heart, is an exclusive campus attended by the children of the city's wealthy and influential elite. Mixing with the cream of New York

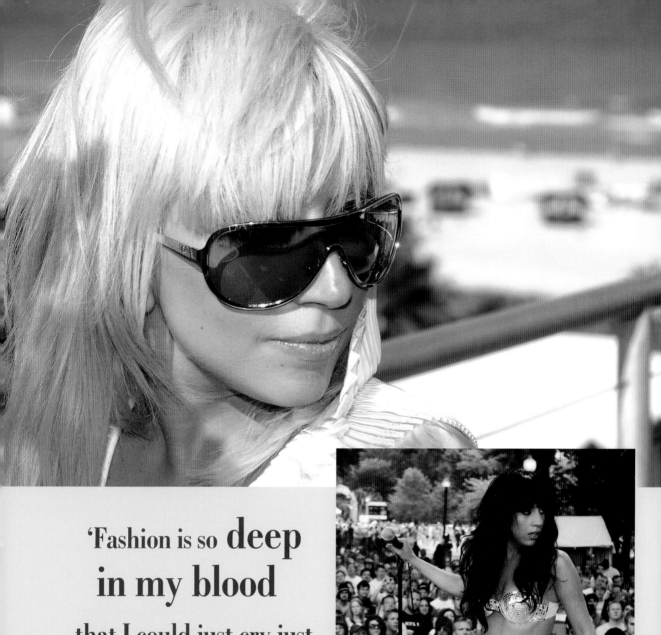

'Fashion is so **deep in my blood** that I could just cry just sitting here talking to you about it.'

Previous page: Queen of the night: Gaga rocks the 'fashion road kill' gown created for her by Giorgio Armani at the 2010 VMAs. Above: Miami vice: Gaga soaks up the sun on a penthouse balcony in Miami's South Beath, March 2008. Right: Brunette ambition: Gaga's homemade disco-ball bra makes its debut at Lollapalooza fest, Chicago, August 2007.

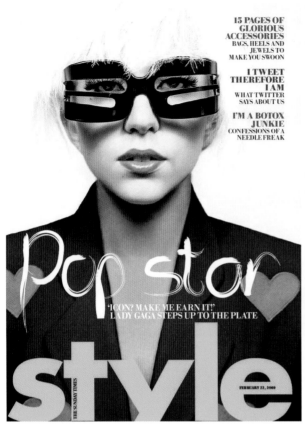

15 PAGES OF
GLORIOUS
ACCESSORIES
BAGS, HEELS AND
JEWELS TO
MAKE YOU SWOON

I TWEET
THEREFORE
I AM
WHAT TWITTER
SAYS ABOUT US

I'M A BOTOX
JUNKIE
CONFESSIONS OF A
NEEDLE FREAK

♥ Pop star ♥

'ICON? MAKE ME EARN IT!'
LADY GAGA STEPS UP TO THE PLATE

style

THE SUNDAY TIMES   FEBRUARY 22, 2009

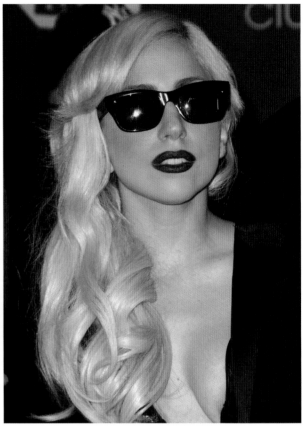

Above: Gaga flaunts her collection of smoking shades – on the cover of Sunday Times Style *and at an LA signing in November 2009. Opposite: Flights of fancy: Gaga touches down at Berlin Airport, clad in an elaborate cut-away top, September 2009.*

society (including the ultra-glam heiress Nicky Hilton), Gaga quickly learned the importance of whichever face she chose to show to the world.

Joking that her annual prom resembled nothing so much as a Ralph Lauren runway, Gaga opened up about her classmates live on-air with London's Capitol Radio. 'They're very pretty and very, very clean,' she confided. 'But, you know, it's impressive to be *that* perfect all the time. I was always a weird girl in school, who did theatre [. . .] and came with lots of red lipstick on or my hair perfectly curled, or whatever I was doing to get attention. It's funny as it's almost like they were there to make me aware, because so much of what I do now is that I try to twist my world into the commercial community, so I guess they've been quite an influence on me. Not them in particular, but the idea of the self-proclaimed artist.' In the game of 'poker-facing', the material girls of the Sacred Heart virtually wrote the rules. Never again would Stefani underestimate the power of superficial appearances.

A decade on, Lady Gaga – Stefani's own freakishly beautiful hybrid creation, comprising a little of each of her most beloved icons, twisted to hell and spliced together – is no less 'perfect' than the preening misses of the Convent.

> 'I was always a **weird girl in school,** who did theatre and came with lots of red lipstick on or my hair perfectly curled, or whatever I was doing to get attention.'

'I THINK WHAT MADONNA AND I SHARE IS THAT WE ARE BOTH FEARLESS.'

[Matt Williams – Gaga's trusted stylist and Haus of Gaga mainstay], "I have never seen a braided hair garment." So, I said, "I want it to be an ode to Madonna with a little bit of a conical bra!'"

Fortunately, Gaga's admiration for the reigning queen of pop seems entirely mutual. 'I see myself in Lady Gaga,' Madge told *Rolling Stone.* 'When I saw her, she didn't have a lot of money for her production. She's got holes in her fishnets and there's mistakes everywhere. It was kind of a mess, but I can see that she has that IT factor. It's nice to see that at a raw stage.'

Love at first sight it may have been, but since the show described by Madonna, baby Gaga – backed by the Haus of Gaga, her team of dream designers and technological wizards – has taken giant strides forward. These days, Lady G's tattered fishnets may remain, but those provide the only visible holes in an otherwise flawlessly executed stage show. And, while her style may be partly inspired by Madge's classic looks, there's almost always a contemporary twist – whether it involves a dash of Heidi chic and one strategically placed plait, or something altogether more shocking. On the evening of the MuchMusic Awards, the nation watched Gaga 'make my tits blow up [. . .] live on television', against the better judgement of everyone in the Haus.

'I called up Matty,' the hyper star revealed, 'and he's like, "I can't do that! We can't put pyro on you." And I said, "Yes, you can. Figure it out." Then I hung up on him and he called me back later with this really nerdy explanation as to how we could do it.' Anyone who's witnessed the awesome spectacle of Gaga's flame-throwing bra – a show-stopping device with the potential to spit out sparks at perilously close range – will know that Williams delivered everything Lady G wanted and more, proving that whatever your

Opposite: Pyromania: Gaga test drives her fire-cracking new bra – as crafted by geekily gifted Haus mate, Matty Dada. Right: Put your paws up: Gaga rocks the Today *show, July 2010.*

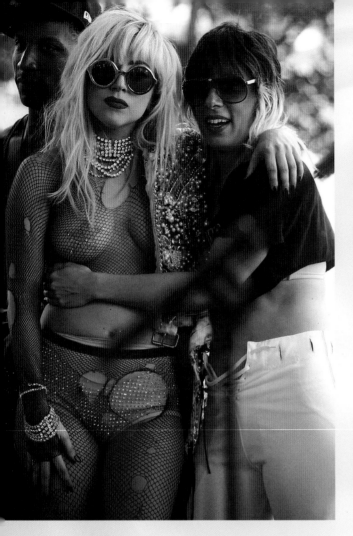

Above: Backstage with Lady Starlight, the crazily creative go-go dancer who was Angie Bowie to Gaga's David, Lollapalooza 2010. Opposite: Taste the rainbow. Gaga dazzles onstage at Brixton Academy, July 2009. 'Because that's where your fame lives . . . my luminosity, my constant flashing light.'

American women, we both started out in the New York underground scene and we both became famous when we dyed our hair blonde' (though, ironically enough, in Stefani's case it was the determination not to be mistaken for a pint-sized Amy Winehouse impersonator that first inspired her to reach for the bleach) – the true likeness between these two artists may run deeper than you think. 'I think what Madonna and I share is that we are both fearless,' Gaga mused in an interview with the *Sunday Times*. 'We both have a lot of nerve.'

In truth, Madge was not the only fearless female in Gaga's life. While 20-year-old Stefani was still honing her style on the New York club circuit – playing virtually anywhere she could get a gig – she met the charismatic Lady Starlight, a hard-rocking DJ and burlesque dancer who'd already created precisely the kind of wild onstage persona the arts-school drop-out wanted for herself. Convinced that the conventional training on offer at the Tisch was not for her ('everybody did the same shit – super boring!') Stefani was in desperate need of some direction – and Lady Starlight was the one to show her the way. It was a collaboration that led to the creation of Lady Gaga – and some seriously good times!

The stereotypical Catholic schoolgirl gone wild, Gaga's newfound freedom was proving dangerously addictive. 'I was wearing a leopard g-string at a nightclub with Lady Starlight,' Gaga reveals. 'And we were wearing Indian headdresses dancing to "Run to the Hills" by Iron Maiden. [My father] just thought I was completely nuts! He didn't get it and I don't know if I really got it.'

But, whether Gaga 'got it' or not, her days as a surreally sexy, metal-headed squaw were enough to make Stefani realise that 'all that ever holds somebody back is fear. For a minute I had fear. Then I went into the dressing room and shot my

opinion of Gaga, she's a free-minded force to be reckoned with, her head chock-full of ideas and her cherished team all but incapable of telling her 'no'.

Sparking as many comparisons with Rosie the robot (sassy maid to the Jetson family) as queen Madge, Gaga has forged an iconic new look that's all her own. Even those who've never heard Gaga's infectious brand of pop couldn't fail to recognise her at this crucial moment in her fire-cracking show. After all, Madonna's corsetry was often provocative, but never pyrotechnic.

While Gaga herself is well aware of the superficial similarities – 'we're both Italian-

'All that ever **holds somebody back** is fear. For a minute I had fear. Then I went into the dressing room and **shot my fear** in the face.'

fear in the face.' Without fear, the possibilities for Gaga are endless – as Lady Starlight appreciates. 'It's really more of an attitude towards fashion and performance that I've inspired in her [Lady Gaga] . . . of just, go all the way and just go for it. Do it . . . and then, do it all the way at 150 miles per hour!'

Burning up the stage with Lady Starlight, Gaga had her first intoxicating taste of life as a performance artist. 'I actually never really thought about it like that until I started working with Lady Starlight,' recalls Gaga. 'One day she was like, "It's not really a concert and it's not really a show, it's performance art. What you're doing is not just singing; it's art." And once she pointed that out to me . . . I just started analysing that more and researching to try to take it in a different direction.'

Starlight's brand of 'performance art' was precisely the creative outlet baby Gaga had been searching for. Finally, it was okay for Stefani to let her inner freak shine through. Indeed, in Lady Starlight's thrilling world of drag queens and party gods, a wacky sense of style was fast becoming the strongest card Stefani had to play. As Gaga stated years later in no uncertain terms, 'You're only as strong of a woman as a presence on the street with your fashion, that's the first way that you stake your strength as a woman.'

Though Stefani's constant gigging left her little time for boyfriends, this was nonetheless the moment she embarked on a lasting love affair . . . with an enviable collection of cripplingly cute high-heeled shoes. 'I was a go-go dancer, so I like to wear stripper shoes,' she explained on a guided tour of her cavernous wardrobe backstage on the Monster Ball tour, adding that 'we buy very inexpensive shoes and then we reinforce them' – a revelation that must have set a million little-monster hearts aflutter. With a little imagination and copious amounts of PVC glue, Gaga's towering, glitzy heels – almost as magical as Dorothy's ruby slippers – may not be so far out of reach as you'd think.

Opposite: Pearly queen: Gaga shines as the dreamy white face of Mac's Viva Glam campaign, New York City, February 2010. Right: Stairway to heaven: Gaga treads the red carpet at the 2010 Grammy Awards, clad in dazzling diamanté heels.

As well as adding inches to Stefani's height and inspiring her to leave her pants at home (with a vast wardrobe of figure-hugging leotards and cute neon bikinis to choose from, it seems Gaga hasn't missed them), you'd be forgiven for assuming Lady Starlight was the one to have completed Stefani's new stage-name. But at least some of the credit for this must go to Gaga's ex-songwriting partner, Rob Fusari. Even now, Stefani can call to mind the exact moment when 'Lady Gaga' was born. 'It came from the Queen song, "Radio Ga Ga". I used to perform that song at the piano, doing these really theatrical performances where I would do hand choreography and then slam my fingers back down on the piano and I would wear lingerie . . . and he [Rob] just told me, "You're so Ga Ga, you're so Freddie Mercury." And I was like, "You mean Radio Ga Ga?" I just thought the name was so fitting, so I kept it [. . .] it just kind of stuck.'

Of course, anyone familiar with Mercury's riveting presence onstage can see how 'Gaga' was a perfect fit for the pop princess in-waiting. Though the Queen front-man sadly passed away in 1991, his epic performances will never be forgotten. Mercury by name and mercurial by nature, Freddie was a natural-born showman who never tired of reinventing himself from the outside-in. For each of Queen's good-time anthems, there's a groundbreaking video to match, featuring Mercury in one of his wildest guises – from the long-lashed angel (clad in a white satin cat-suit) who played 'Bohemian Rhapsody' to the moustachioed strutting sportsman whose baseball cap appeared to be sprouting its own pair of horns (apparently Freddie was as much of a mad-hatter as his 'Gaga' namesake) to the frustrated housewife who sang, 'I Want to Break Free'.

The sight of Freddie sashaying around his living room in drag – flashing the tops of his lacy stockings and brandishing his feather duster like a domestic goddess – was more than certain bigoted viewers could stomach. Back when it premiered in 1984, the film's playful cross-dressing, gender-bending concept was an altogether more daring one than it is now.

'I guess I'm trying to push the limits, push the boundaries as much as I can,' commented Lady Gaga, on the subject of her own flirtation with all things androgynous. (Gaga herself has created her own suave male alter ego and is never afraid to disguise her feminine charms with pumped-up shoulder pads and power dressing.) Yet, to a certain extent, pioneering artists like Freddie smoothed the way for her decades earlier – for which Gaga remains eternally grateful: 'Without Bowie and Queen and Madonna I don't know that I would have figured out how to bring together theatre and pop music,' she mused. 'For me Bowie and Queen and mad studying their work was a way to really be myself, and really integrate all of the theatrics and the things that are important for me in a pop show and how it makes sense to lots of young people.'

And yet, on Gaga's own personal list of inspiring individuals, there's one name to be reeled off before all others. At the mention of eccentric English rocker David Bowie, the garrulous Lady Gaga lights up like she'll never require her electrified TV glasses again. Ensconced on a sofa with television presenter Alexa Chung, she began to gush, 'I used to sit in my apartment for hours and do his make-up on myself over and over again!' Of course, glam-rock chameleon David Bowie has changed his 'make-up' – and, indeed, his complete persona

'I guess I'm trying to push the limits, push the boundaries as much as I can.'

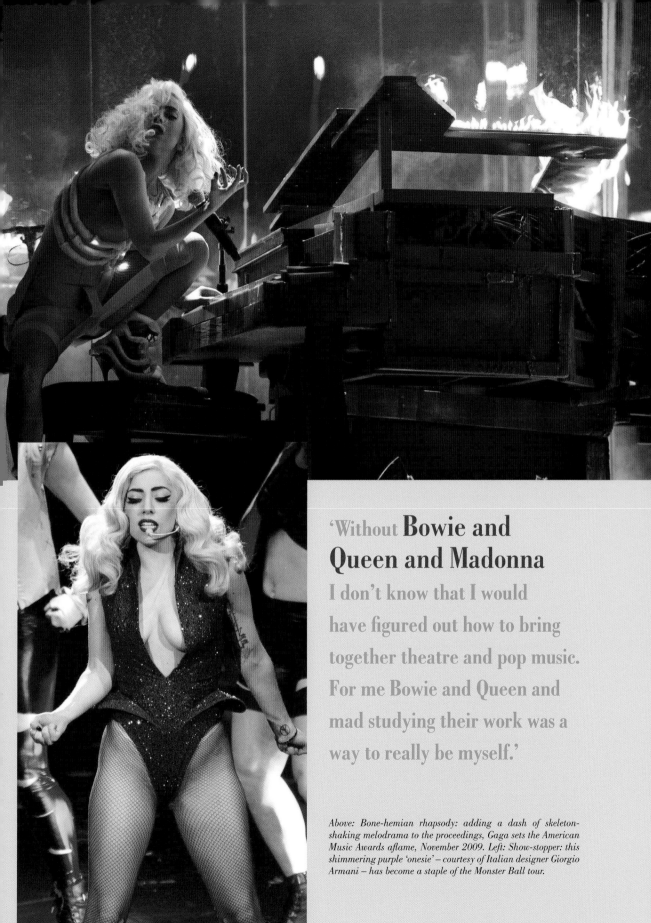

'Without **Bowie and Queen and Madonna** I don't know that I would have figured out how to bring together theatre and pop music. For me Bowie and Queen and mad studying their work was a way to really be myself.'

Above: Bone-hemian rhapsody: adding a dash of skeleton-shaking melodrama to the proceedings, Gaga sets the American Music Awards aflame, November 2009. Left: Show-stopper: this shimmering purple 'onesie' – courtesy of Italian designer Giorgio Armani – has become a staple of the Monster Ball tour.

– more often and more drastically than most people could ever dream of. Yet, with her eye for rainbow colour, glam and glitz, there can be little doubt as to which of Bowie's intriguing incarnations has caught Gaga's imagination.

Back in the seventies, David Bowie 'went totally out the window' – by his own admission – only to be replaced by Ziggy Stardust, a flame-haired demigod who was beautiful, but not entirely of this world. In fact, he was an alien saviour, sent down from the sky to make Earth's final days a little less bleak. This was the twisted tale concocted by Bowie for his rock opera, *The Rise and Fall of Ziggy Stardust and the Spiders from Mars*, in any case. And thanks to some clever styling by Bowie's wife, Angela, it was entirely believable. As pop legend has it, Bowie's outrageous new alter ego began as a daydream on the train, his name borrowed from a tailor's shop called Ziggy's. According to Bowie, 'I thought, "Well, this whole thing is gonna be about clothes," so it was my own little joke calling him Ziggy. Ziggy Stardust was a real compilation of things.'

A 'little joke' is how it may have started out, but when it came to dressing Ziggy, Bowie's approach was deadly serious. Glimpsed strutting his stuff on stages across the UK, Ziggy's attire was never anything less than out of this world. Drawn from a well-stocked wardrobe of Technicolor cat-suits, shimmering stardust pants and impossibly high palm-tree platforms, his outlandish attire spoke of another dimension altogether. 'Everyone became real quiet,' remembers Rodney Bingenheimer, an awe-struck DJ in attendance at one of Ziggy's legendary sell-out shows in Santa Monica. 'It was like seeing music from the future.'

Over a decade before Stefani was born, Ziggy Stardust materialised like a pale-faced premonition of some of Gaga's most spellbinding looks. Turn Ziggy's iconic 'Rites of Spring'

costume on its head – the hypnotic, curving lines of this creation by Kansai Yamamoto make Bowie look less like a human being and more like a gargantuan PVC pear (his legs completely absorbed by two huge bell-bottom trouser legs) – and you'd be left with something resembling the crazed lilac jacket rocked by Lady Gaga at Lollapalooza. Clashing with her daffodil-yellow locks, the giant, padded shoulders of her jacket transformed Gaga from tiny dancer to androgynous, angular powerhouse in an instant. But even when she shed the jacket – along with her pair of glitzy, fly-eye shades – Gaga looked no more like Stefani. Clad in a latex leopard leotard that clung to her like a second skin, she cut a mesmerising, feline figure – a vamped-up Thundercat come to show the masses the next step in fashion's ongoing evolution.

'I love David Bowie . . . he is the reason I make music.'

Back in the 1970s, Bowie's woodland creature playsuit was a similarly groundbreaking number. Adorned with cute white rabbits, the suit lived up to its name completely, demonstrating much the same penchant for kitsch couture that's shaped the style of Bowie's twenty-first-century equivalent, as well as proving that Gaga was far from the first performer to opt for a daring 'no pants' look.

Such is the similarity that, in the video for 'Just Dance', Gaga decorated one cheek with a shimmering, blue lightning bolt – an emblem

Opposite: Shut up and drive: a fly-eyed vision in purple, Gaga lets her pumped-up shoulder pads do the talking, Lollapalooza 2010.

THROUGH THE LOOKING GLAS

that's always been synonymous with Ziggy Stardust – in open homage to Bowie's stellar style. 'It's a tribute to Bowie,' she explained with a shy smile. 'It's my first video; I really wanted to stake my claim as an artist.' In another interview, she stated simply: 'I love David Bowie . . . he is the reason I make music.'

But after stepping into Ziggy's crippling PVC platforms, Gaga is already feeling the sinister undertones of Bowie's spaced-out style. In his tale of glam-rock decadence, there's a twist – Ziggy Stardust's fall from grace. In Gaga's own mind – just as her idol experienced decades earlier – the line between art and life has already begun to blur. On the street and on the stage, she looks the same. These days, Stefani's own parents are calling her 'Gaga'. Though the unstoppable Lady Gaga began as a character, her changing style begs the question: exactly who is playing whom?

'I thought I might as well take Ziggy out to interviews as well,' Bowie told *Rolling Stone*

> 'You're only as strong of a woman as a presence on the street with your fashion, that's the first way that you stake your strength as a woman.'

back in 1987, reflecting on what it is to discard the clothes, but never the character. '"Why leave him on the stage? Why not complete the canvas?" Looking back it was completely absurd. It became very dangerous. I really did have doubts about my sanity . . . I think I put myself very dangerously near the line. Not in a physical sense, but definitely in a mental sense.'

'I packaged a totally credible plastic rock star – much better than any sort of Monkees fabrication. My plastic rocker was much more plastic than anybody's,' he added. And though Ziggy Stardust provides the glittering blueprint for Lady Gaga ('we're plastic, but we still have fun,' yelled Gaga in an eerie echo of Bowie's words), Gaga's style is about so much more than straightforward mimicry. Despite her exhibitionist tendencies, there's more beneath the surface that you'll never see.

Opposite: Star in her eyes? Lady G channels David Bowie's decadent 'plastic rocker' live onstage at the 2010 Grammy Awards.

'A SEQUIN, TO ME, IS REPRESENTATIVE OF HAVING A GOOD TIME.'

Mother Monster will always be willing to give her little monsters just a little of what they're craving – fleeting glimpses of her innermost fears, morbid fascinations and obsessive dreams . . . the darkest, deepest, sickest secrets of Stefani Germanotta, tattooed on Gaga's sleeve for all to see.

Indeed, whatever else she's borrowed from other artists, this darkened element can't help but bleed through into her look – quite literally, in the case of her gore-laden performance at the VMAs in 2009. 'I'm struggling with all sorts of things, but that's the nature of being an artist,' she revealed in an intriguing interview with Vibe TV. 'I think that when you stop struggling, that's when your music starts to suck, so I'm sort of holding on to my solitude and wrestling with all of my thoughts and I guess you could say that all the years of drive and ambition and the dream were like a mask for the feelings . . . now my fears are running out of me, because the mask is off.'

Whether she's battling her fears every night onstage (in the form of a gargantuan angler fish with flaming lamps for eyes), decorating her eyes, clothes and accessories with copious amounts of glitter ('a sequin, to me, is representative of having a good time'), or staging the 'murder' of a certain crimson-clad princess at the hands of the paparazzi (of her shocking VMA performance, she explained, 'That was a commentary about Princess Diana and about being a martyr to fame and how she touched my life and my mother's life when I was so young . . . the red lace was meant to symbolise my eternal martyrdom'), there's a certain element of Gaga's fashion that is inspired by no one.

Formidable eighties icon Grace Jones (another of Gaga's heroes) is, ironically enough, less than

> **'I'm struggling with all sorts of things, but that's the nature of being an artist.'**

impressed by her young successor's look. In an interview with the *Guardian*, she commented curtly, 'Well, you know, I've seen some things she's worn that I've worn and that does kind of piss me off.' Perhaps Jones was thinking of the surreally rigid wimple that she wore in concert with Luciano Pavarotti (teamed with flowing satin bat-wings, it was surely a forebear of Gaga's staple PVC-nun outfit), or the thorny lace headgear she wore on Jonathan Ross's Friday night show back in 2008, reminiscent of the arresting jagged lace crown worn by Gaga at the VMAs? Nevertheless, it seems as though Jones (a former muse of Andy Warhol, the artist whose Factory of beautiful freaks, artists and designers provided the blueprint for Gaga's Haus) has forgotten her own roots as a struggling theatre student all too easily.

In early 2010, Rob Fusari – the ex-lover who gave Gaga her name and helped shape the career of the 'Italian girl guidette' who first came to his door – attempted to sue his former collaborator for what he saw as rightfully his: a considerable cut of the Monster Ball profits. Before the tangled proceedings were complete, he decided to drop the case and walk away. Perhaps because he realised he was on to a loser. Though Fusari himself offered no further comment on the case, Gaga was soon to smash the silence in spectacular style.

'Nobody made me,' she fumed in interview with *Vanity Fair*. 'Nobody fucking made me who I am today. And what is so funny is that everyone that was spitting in my face and treating me like

Opposite left: Lifting her first ever 'moon man' (Best New Artist at the 2009 VMAs), Gaga keeps her poker face under wraps. Opposite right: In the hood: Lady G strikes a pose backstage at MTV's Total Request Live, held in her hometown, New York City, August 2008.

'I guess you could say that all the years of drive and ambition and the dream were like a mask for the feelings.'

'I'm a lion, and **I can't be destroyed**. The things that I have been through, the **things I have seen**, the people I have taken care of . . . I would not take any of it back, because it's made me the writer I am.'

dirt and making me feel so worthless . . . The price that a woman pays for people destroying you over and over again . . . I'm a lion, and I can't be destroyed. The things that I have been through, the things I have seen, the people I have taken care of . . . I would not take any of it back, because it's made me the writer I am. But how dare anyone that treated you like dirt on the bottom of their shoe try to turn around and tell you that they made you? The minute you have a glimpse of sunlight on your lashes, they fuckin' made you that mascara.'

Beneath Gaga's glinting armour, some small part of Stefani still remains – living proof that whatever doesn't kill you will only make you shine. Armed with flawless taste, the guidance of some seriously stylish mentors and an imagination as limitless as her spaced-out wardrobe of delights, Gaga is in complete control of her changing look. And while she may be on a fashion 'journey' with no one but herself, it doesn't mean the rest of humanity can't take a front-row seat and enjoy . . .

Right: Arm candy: Gaga's beloved Hermès handbag makes an appearance at Tokyo airport, April 2010. 'I love small monster, Tokyo love' read the heartfelt message scrawled across the front. Opposite: Shades: Jacks Eyewear store. Adoring minions: model's own. Gaga strikes a pose at Open A.I.R., May 2008.

WHEN THE HEAD RULES THE HEART

'When I wake up in the morning, **I feel just like any other insecure 24-year-old** girl. Then I say, "Bitch, you're Lady Gaga, you get up and walk the walk today."'

Though decoration has always been the That's primary function, historically they have often been worn as status symbols. Be it a king's crown, a gladiator's helmet or a policeman's cap, in times past hats commonly denoted the achievements and authority of the wearer – what they did or didn't have on their head told you who you were dealing with, and how to treat them. These days, however, you don't need to be a queen to wear a crown, nor a moneyed member of the aristocracy to wear a flowering, gilt-edged fascinator (although it certainly helps), and hats are more likely to be representative of a highly developed fashion sense than a social or professional rank. Pop royalty she may be, but Lady Gaga's passion for exotic, elaborate and in some cases literally hair-raising headwear is rooted in a love of the artistry involved, rather than a simple desire to let everyone in the room know who she is (even if that is a beneficial side effect).

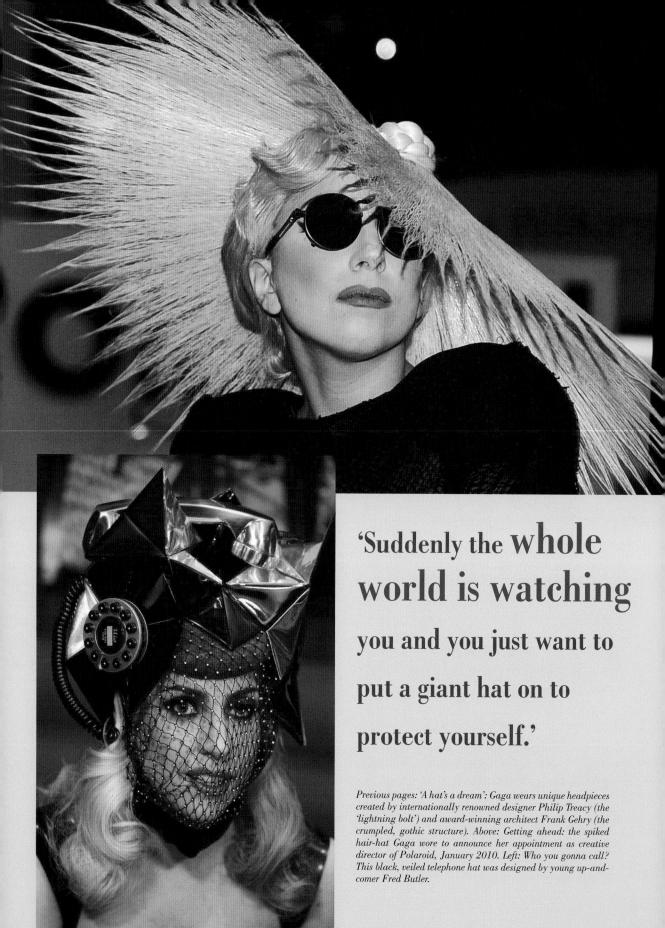

'Suddenly the **whole world is watching** you and you just want to put a giant hat on to protect yourself.'

Previous pages: 'A hat's a dream': Gaga wears unique headpieces created by internationally renowned designer Philip Treacy (the 'lightning bolt') and award-winning architect Frank Gehry (the crumpled, gothic structure). Above: Getting ahead: the spiked hair-hat Gaga wore to announce her appointment as creative director of Polaroid, January 2010. Left: Who you gonna call? This black, veiled telephone hat was designed by young up-and-comer Fred Butler.

Above left: Head in the clouds: this Marie Antoinette-inspired Philip Treacy piece cost a reported £6,000. Above right: Seaside glamour: Gaga attends her London after-show party wearing a bejewelled lobster in March 2010.

From the slick black telephone she chose for *Friday Night with Jonathan Ross* to the spiky sunhat that lit up a Las Vegas Electronics Show – made from nothing but the Lady's own hair, it circled her head like a monstrous blonde sea urchin – to the bejewelled silver lobster that glittered in the paparazzo camera flashes en route to a glitzy London after-party, to the Marie Antoinette-inspired, bulbous candy-floss creation she performed in at the 2010 Brit Awards, Gaga has but one rule when it comes to her hats: 'The bigger the better. The more interesting and outrageous the better.'

For Gaga, fashion comes first, not only as a pivotal accompaniment to her music and performances, but also as a valuable form of protection – one just as essential as her ever-present burly security guards, without whom she is incapable of venturing out into public. 'Everything happened so quickly for me,' she said. 'Suddenly the whole world is watching you and you just want to put a giant hat on to protect yourself.' She has compared some of her more dramatic outfits to 'armour', and revealed that her hats are both a definitive style statement and a particularly symbolic shield. 'It is a nice barrier. For me, it keeps the devil away. I always like when I have a hat that's big enough to keep people away at pretentious parties. It's protection. It's a sense of home away from home.'

Her captivating, extravagant silver crustacean and Marie Antoinette hats were just two of the devil-thwarting homes away from home that were made for Gaga by Philip Treacy, whose work she became infatuated with after commissioning him to create pieces for her Monster Ball tour. 'What

Above left: Behind the mask: wearing a jewel-encrusted Erickson Beamon piece, Gaga leaves Manhattan's Carnegie Hall in May 2010. Above right: In bloom: Gaga attends the Mac Viva Glam launch in elaborate floral headwear, London, March 2010. Opposite: Très chic: Gaga adopts an elegant porcelain-doll look in London, April 2009.

'I always like when I have a hat that's big enough to keep people away at pretentious parties. **It's protection.** It's a sense of home away from home.'

I like about a Philip Treacy hat is that they're like nobody else's,' she said of the milliner's unique designs. 'They protect me in a different way, a social canopy.'

Treacy, whose celebrity clientele includes Duchess of Cornwall Camilla Parker Bowles, *Sex and the City* actress Sarah Jessica Parker and notoriously eccentric singer (and Gaga's own kooky style queen) Grace Jones, has

become Gaga's go-to source for seductively unconventional headgear whenever she feels the need to reaffirm her status as a fashion icon. 'I suppose he's done quite a few items for her before, but he's just started doing a number of hats for her for big events,' a spokesperson for the designer revealed. 'She has quite a different style, and she likes what Philip creates. The designs are time-consuming, but Philip can do anything.'

The sparkling multi-dimensional lightning-bolt hat Gaga wore during her victorious appearance at the 2010 Grammys was one of the first Treacy-Gaga collaborations to make

'WHAT I LIKE ABOUT A **PHILIP TREACY** HAT IS THAT THEY'RE **LIKE NOBODY ELSE'S.**'

Above: Strike a bow: Like her career, Lady G's hair bows (an early Haus of Gaga invention) keep getting bigger, better and evermore colourful. Opposite: Gaga goes On the Record *in Jean Paul Gaultier at Fuse TV studios, November 2009.*

'The more interesting and outrageous the better.'

headlines the world over, and since then their association has been the object of much media speculation, not least when it was announced that Gaga had sent in her résumé in the hope of scoring a training placement at Treacy's company.

'She has expressed an interest,' Treacy revealed, 'so we're going to check out her sewing skills and see if she's good enough, you never know!' Even the biggest pop star on the planet, it seemed, was not exempt from the rigorous selection process involved in getting a gig with one of the world's

most famous hat-makers. Whether Gaga's hat-design internship ever actually happened was never confirmed, though between constant international touring and her unwavering belief that – wherever the place, whatever the hour – underdressing simply *isn't* an option, it's hard to imagine how she'd find the time.

Philip Treacy, himself no stranger to celebrity or eccentricity, spoke about the creative relationship he shares with the new first lady of fashion. 'Lady Gaga is definitely interesting, but she chooses from what I make,' he explained. 'She's a great character, she loves hats and she is a very exciting customer because she is the hat wearer du jour, no?'

Since the late eighties, when he was discovered as a student at London's Royal College of Art by then-*Tatler* style editor Isabella Blow (herself an iconic devotee of outlandish headwear and one of Gaga's key fashion antecedents), Treacy has enjoyed huge success in the fashion industry and maintained an enviably high-profile career for over two decades. 'Hats are a personal choice,'

FLARE

CANADA'S FASHION AUTHORITY

EXCLUSIVE!

Lady Gaga

"Fashion saved my life"

EASY
DAY TO
NIGHT
Hair &
makeup tips

HOLIDAY GLAMOUR

THE LITTLE BLACK DRESS FRENCH CHIC, PARTY SHINE & THE TUXEDO

$3.99
DEC 2009
FLARE.COM

LADY GAGA
THE REMIX

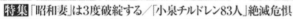

特集 「昭和妻」は3度破綻する／「小泉チルドレン83人」絶滅危惧

AER

'09.8.3
No.34定価380円
アエラ

Left: For a July 2010 appearance on NBC's the Today *show, Gaga appeared in this pearl-embellished, feathered headpiece by Keko Hainswheeler. Above: Flower of the orient: Gaga wore this one-of-a-kind Balmung headgear during a Mac Viva Glam-sponsored performance in Tokyo, April 2010.*

he said, 'and really give a person the chance to assert their sense of independence [. . .] Women who are conservative dressers can add something extra with a hat. Hat wearers are really misunderstood because people assume they are extroverts when actually they are shy and hats give them confidence.' Treacy's words ring all too true. While she's far from a conservative dresser, Gaga has revealed that – beneath the Kermit coats and hair bows – she's just as prone to feelings of insecurity and vulnerability as the next person. 'When I wake up in the morning, I feel just like any other insecure 24-year-old girl,' she told *Rolling Stone*. 'Then I say, "Bitch, you're Lady Gaga, you get up and walk the walk today."'

Philip Treacy's statement-making, often gravity-defying creations are notorious on the international fashion scene, combining the skill of millinery with the artistry of sculpture, and winning him work with design houses including Versace, Chanel, Valentino, Thierry Mugler, Givenchy and Alexander McQueen. Lady Gaga favours Treacy's couture hats, which are hand-finished, can take as long as 100 hours to make, and cost upwards of £5,000. The cloud-puff Marie Antoinette piece Gaga wore to the Brit Awards, for example, was said to have cost over £6,000, and was certainly worth its weight in column inches. ('Lady Gaga wins a hat-trick of prizes,' punned the *Telegraph*'s headline.)

'For me, when I'm thinking about either designing a piece or choosing a piece to wear, I think about a shape,' Gaga explained cryptically. 'If you, as a designer, your aesthetic were to walk through a wooden door, what shape would

'For me, when I'm thinking about either designing a piece or choosing a piece to wear, **I think about a shape.**'

it leave?' And, like an overexcitable Looney Tunes character leaving their silhouette smashed through woodwork, Lady G's chosen hats leave a permanent, glitter-embossed mark upon the public consciousness.

The face-obscuring wreath of white feathers Gaga wore when sitting in the audience at the MTV's 2009 Video Music Awards – a cross between an Eskimo's hood and a pristine bird's nest – was classic Treacy. Ornate, bizarrely beautiful and deliciously impractical, it was a perfect example of the designer's assertion that 'glamour is the ultimate accessory'. Of his design process, he has said that 'the personality of the wearer and the hat makes the hat. I always design a hat with a wearer in mind, otherwise it's an inanimate object . . . It's a hat, but a hat's a dream. It's an accessory of rebellion in a way.' It should then come as no surprise that the hats he designed with someone as enigmatic and visually arresting as Lady Gaga in mind have proven to be among his most accomplished and beautifully realised. Both Treacy and Gaga are in the business of creating dreams and selling fantasies, and together they've produced a succession of opulent, artful outfits that have successfully stirred the imagination of millions.

Right: En vogue: An immaculately outfitted Gaga works it for the cameras at the Dome 47 music show in Mannheim, Germany, August 2008.

While Philip Treacy might be the best-known hat designer Lady Gaga employs, he's certainly not the only one. Since her ascendancy to the upper echelons of the fashion world, Gaga has emerged as a valuable supporter of young, often lesser-known designers, not least those capable of creating outrageous headwear.

Nasir Mazhar, responsible for the intricately constructed golden 'orb' headpiece that Gaga has worn on several occasions, including a shoot for *V* magazine, is another 'hatter' (as he refers to himself) championed by the singer, and one who shares similar creative drives: 'I try to create a world for myself,' he declares, 'but I know real life seeps in and has its effect.'

Alex Noble, a London-based designer in his early twenties, constructed the huge feathered horns – almost as tall as the singer herself – that Gaga wore during the Monster Ball tour.

Right: Deer in the headlights: Gaga gets into the festive spirit during a December 2009 visit to London. French design duo Mouton Collet created this furry helmet using real deer horns.

Amongst other things, he was also responsible for the red bondage strap suit from the 'Bad Romance' video, and said, 'Lady Gaga and her team are perfect to work for as anything goes, with everything you do you have to push it more and more, and stay ahead of how their vision is changing. But generally it's a really enjoyable and creative process.' Mouton Collet, a French design duo 'inspired by the vegetal and animal world', created Gaga's fluffy white antler helmet using real deer horns, and the S&M-inspired spiked helmets from the 'Alejandro' video. Piers Atkinson, a milliner who trained under iconic designer Zandra Rhodes, made Gaga's charcoal felt beret with crystal mesh veil. 'I invent stories,' he says. 'My hats are characters.' And who better to take these lovingly crafted characters onto the world stage than Lady Gaga?

A young British fashion-design graduate who has produced one-off commissions for bands including the Gossip, La Roux and Sigur Ros, Fred Butler designed the infamous blue geometric telephone hat that Nicola Formichetti ordered for the 'Telephone' video. 'I always love the notion of capturing a moment for future generations,' Butler said. 'I think that Lady Gaga is singlehandedly amassing an amazing collection of outfits by emerging talents that will make a fascinating museum exhibition one day. To be part of that is very exciting.' Butler also commented on the career-enhancing impact of Gaga's patronage, and how she went from being a virtual unknown to having global recognition in the time it took for the nine-minute video to premiere: 'It has given me an instant international platform that is unparalleled. The attention I receive is very bizarre, from Lady Gaga fans stalking me on Facebook, to people calling me asking for replica hats. She [Gaga] has singlehandedly elevated the profile of all the emerging designers in London and that is a great credit to her.'

Above: Hair today, gone tomorrow: Gaga performs in wigmaker Charlie Le Mindu's multi-tiered 'hair monster' outfit at the Lollapalooza Festival, Chicago, August 2010.

Haus of Gaga stylist Formichetti has introduced Gaga to many members of London's up-and-coming fashion avant garde, 23-year-old wig-maker Charlie Le Mindu among them. Specialising in towering hair structures such as his giant lip wigs and Eiffel Tower headpieces, he has created several wigs and headdresses for Gaga, including the notorious 'hair monster' outfit she performed in on the Monster Ball tour

– a stunning multi-tiered creation in which Gaga looked like the missing link between a high-fashion yeti and *The Addams Family*'s Cousin It. 'The rule is to be as creative as possible,' Le Mindu said, echoing sentiments familiar to little monsters everywhere. 'Lady Gaga wears my wigs a lot and I think she is perfect for them! Her look is fun but really high-end at the same time.'

'There is absolutely no way I'd ever give up my wigs and hats for anything.'

Above: Clawing her way to the top: Gaga and a wide-brimmed hat of epic proportions leave the studios of Good Morning America *in New York following an appearance to promote 'Born This Way', February 2010.*

But it's not only milliners and wigmakers that Gaga turns to when it comes to decorating her head: Frank Gehry, a Pritzker Prize-winning architect well-known for working within the Deconstructivist style, was memorably enlisted by Lady G to create the crumpled, towering headpiece she wore for a benefit performance at the Museum of Contemporary Art in Los Angeles. Gehry claimed to have roughed out the surreal design on his iPhone. 'Since I've never designed a hat before, I was afraid she wouldn't be able to walk,' he told the *New Yorker*. 'I did have an idea that involved people with sticks holding it up, walking behind her. I didn't know how far I could go with this thing.' The final crushed black-and-grey piece Gaga performed in was compared by some critics to the metallic, famously contorted Los Angeles Walt Disney Concert Hall – one of Gehry's signature buildings.

Whether the pieces taking centre stage on Lady Gaga's endlessly photographed head are made by unknown fashionistas, up-and-coming designers, world-class milliners or internationally famous architects, she assures her little monsters that at least one thing is certain: 'There is absolutely no way I'd ever give up my wigs and hats for anything.' And nor, indeed, would we want her to.

'THERE'S ONLY ONE THING
I HATE MORE THAN MONEY …
AND THAT'S THE TRUTH.'

FRACTURING
THE FAIRYTALE

'**C**uriouser and curiouser!' This is Alice's first, hazy impression of Wonderland, and – true to form – Lady Gaga's second appearance on *Friday Night with Jonathan Ross* in March 2010 proved to be no less surreal. This time around, she'd come prepared, armed with a quaint vintage phone-hat that turned out to be more than just a cute accessory. 'Can I ask you about your personal life?' the gossip-hungry Ross wanted to know. But Gaga was not about to let her poker face slip for one moment. Serenely lifting the receiver from her head – where it had been balanced all evening like a precarious crown – Gaga answered her imaginary caller with a polite 'Hello?' before replacing the handset. Between delicate sips of camomile tea, Lady G gave nothing away. 'I asked him [Philip Treacy] to make me this hat,' she told Ross, 'because I wanted to talk to you for the whole interview through the phone, and just in case you weren't nice to me I was going to hang up on you.' Much to Ross's dismay, music and fashion – the singer's burning obsessions – were the only subjects up for discussion that night.

'I haven't really yet, in **my generation**, had sort of a figure that was **an escapist figure for me**, that I could latch on to and have the fantasy of the music and their life **really inspire me.'**

Previous pages: The dark side: Gaga vamps it up in Jean Paul Gaultier (left) and Philip Treacy (right). Above: Promoting Heartbeats in Berlin – a glitzy range of headphones designed by the Lady herself – Gaga opts for a cartoon-cute bob, September 2009. Left: Pretty in pink: Gaga rocks a fun 'n' flirty puff-ball dress backstage at the Brit Awards, London, 2009.

'I haven't really yet, in my generation, had sort of a figure that was an escapist figure for me, that I could latch on to and have the fantasy of the music and their life really inspire me,' she reflected, apparently overlooking the most mesmerising contemporary 'escapist figure' she could have wished for – herself.

'I like to create this atmosphere for my fans where they feel like they have a **freak in me** to hang out with and they **don't feel alone.'**

In recent years, the once-mousy Stefani has grown into a quirky fashion queen, hell-bent on giving pop its most extreme makeover yet. 'I'm just trying to change the world, one sequin at a time,' explained Lady G, with a flutter of her lashes. And with Mother Monster on the scene, the drab, uninspiring idols of Stefani's childhood are fading fast . . .

At the very bottom of the rabbit hole, Alice (the prim Victorian miss in Lewis Carroll's novel, *Alice's Adventures in Wonderland*) uncovers a beguiling world of beauty, where the rules of logic no longer apply. When the contrary becomes ordinary, all things are possible, and – as any little monster will testify – it's something akin to a real-life version of Carroll's savage garden that Lady Gaga has created for her fans.

In an interview with Ellen DeGeneres, Gaga explained, 'The whole point of what I do – the Monster Ball, the music, the performance-art aspect of it – is I want to create a space for my fans where they can feel free and they can celebrate, because I didn't fit in in high school and I felt

Right: Bloomin' lovely: at the grand unveiling of her Heartbeat headphones, Gaga stole the spotlight in ruched gold silk, New York, September 2009.

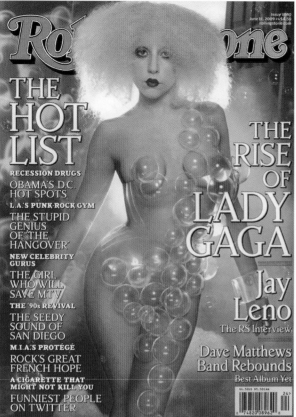

like a freak. So, I like to create this atmosphere for my fans where they feel like they have a freak in me to hang out with and they don't feel alone.' Sadly, 'fitting in' is still an unlikely dream in the minds of many of Gaga's little monsters. And so Mother Monster works tirelessly to provide the next best thing, adding an inclusive dash of rainbow-colour to today's pop scene.

The first time she graced the cover of *Rolling Stone* (back in 2009), Gaga was shot by infamous fashion photographer David LaChapelle, posed against a hot-pink backdrop and immersed in a miniature storm of rainbow bubbles. 'New York Doll' read the swirling headline. And with her cherry lips, ebony lashes and shiny plastic dress, this was exactly how Gaga looked. But this was more than just an exercise in sweet-wrapper chic. As always in Gagaland, it was dress-age with a message. 'I can have hit records all day, but who cares?' Gaga wanted to know. 'A year from now, I could go away, and people might say,

Above left: Gaga brings bubble world to Rolling Stone, *June 2009. Above right and opposite: Forever blowing bubbles: Gaga's frothy attire (seen here in Sydney and Boston) was inspired by a cute one-piece by Hussein Chalayan. Gaga accessorises with one gargantuan glowing piano.*

"Gosh, whatever happened to that girl who never wore pants?" But how wonderfully memorable thirty years from now when they say, "Do you remember Gaga and her bubbles?" Because, for a minute, everybody in that room will forget every sad, painful thing in their lives, and they'll just live in my bubble world.'

And 'bubble world' – a fun, safe space of pure fashion indulgence – is entirely preferable to the mundane alternative, as anyone who's been tuning into hit documentary series *Double Exposure* will realise. Gaga appeared on the show in a cascading gown made from nothing but Hello Kitty dolls – heaped together in a plush mountain of pink silk and white faces – looking like a punked-up Barbie doll. Perched on a

'FOR A MINUTE, EVERYBODY IN THAT ROOM WILL FORGET EVERY SAD, PAINFUL THING IN THEIR LIVES, AND THEY'LL JUST LIVE IN MY BUBBLE WORLD.'

Opposite: Barbie gone gaga? Lady G says 'hello' to a multitude of kitties as a guest on US series, Double Exposure, *July 2010. Above: Beyond the veil . . . in Gaga's world of ghoulish glam, every day is Halloween, 1 November 2009, New York City.*

'We got the throne, the cats all over her! This is Queen Gaga reigning the world from her pop temple!'

throne in an elegant marble chamber, her eyelids fluttered like butterflies, painted with a second set of anime eyes. The illusion was startlingly beautiful. Her hair, too, looked positively delicious – teased into a candyfloss cloud and topped off with yet another miniature cat.

'This is gonna be incredible,' gushed Markus Klinko, one of the photographers behind Gaga's feline fancy. 'It's going to be very Queen Elizabeth . . . we got the throne, the cats all over her! This is Queen Gaga reigining the world from her pop temple!' And the end result certainly didn't disappoint. When 'Queen Gaga' delivered her final verdict, she

couldn't keep the smile from her pastel lips. 'That's insane,' she laughed, looking like the latest girl to stumble down Lewis Carroll's rabbit hole.

Minutes later, Gaga made her way down the sweeping marble staircase after yet another costume change. 'We have to move quickly for this next shot,' photographer Indrani urged, though Gaga seemed to be struggling to move at all – even with Matty Dada's strong arm for support. Dripping with Swarovski crystals, her glinting dress gave her the appearance of an impossibly heavy human chandelier. 'Lady Gaga is wearing a crystal dress that has sharp edges and wires sticking out everywhere!' Indrani revealed anxiously, as Gaga soon realised ('it looks amazing but it's *so* uncomfortable').

Despite her professionalism – and her pledge

Above: Till death do us part: veiled in snowy lace, Gaga's a haunting vision in white at the 2009 Video Music Awards. Opposite: Some enchanted evening: Gaga casts her spell upon LA's Museum of Contemporary Art – with a little help from this dusky-rose piano by Damien Hirst, November 2009.

'Your career will never wake up and tell you that it doesn't love you anymore.'

to dress like a fairytale princess at all times – the weight of the dress under the hot studio lights was clearly becoming too much to take. 'Okay, I've got to sit down,' she eventually interrupted the team of squabbling stylists. 'I'm gonna pass out. I just need a minute to rest if that's alright.' But, in Gaga's wonderland, the ends always justify the means.

Certain journalists were shocked to learn that the quirky fashion queen is yearning for a more conventional future than you might expect. 'I want a husband and children,' Gaga admits. 'In eight to ten years, I want to have babies for my dad to hold, grandkids. I want to have a husband who loves and supports me, the way anyone else does.' But despite this admission, and rumours that

she recently pledged herself to on-off boyfriend Luc Carl in a moonlit ceremony on the ancient island of Crete, Gaga's words on the subject of her current romantic relationships suggest that her spangled heels remain – as ever – firmly on the ground. 'I would never leave my career for a man right now, and I would never follow a man around,' she stated fiercely. 'Some women choose to follow men and some women choose to follow their dreams. If you're wondering which way to go remember that your career will never wake up and tell you that it doesn't love you anymore.' In Gaga's lyrics, love is portrayed as a dangerously addictive game of poker facing, muffin-bluffin' and double dealing. Lose your heart to your opponent and you can never afford to let it show. 'So you all know, ladies,' Gaga whispered behind the back of one tiny, leather-gloved hand, 'the minute they know you like them, they run!'

Draped in veils of frothy white lace and headed for a glitzy after-show party, Gaga floated gracefully down the red carpet at the 2009 VMAs, gazing out from beneath her voluminous headdress – a romantic yet grandmotherly creation held together by two giant embroidery hoops and winding strings of pearls. Beneath the white veil, Gaga's eyes were still caked in glittering black kohl. Remnants of her heavy stage makeup, these shadows were a sinister reminder of all that had come before. Flashback to the sight of Gaga's tiny frame during her

FRACTURING THE FAIRYTALE

'SOME WOMEN CHOOSE
TO FOLLOW MEN
AND SOME WOMEN
CHOOSE TO FOLLOW
THEIR DREAMS.'

performance, dangling from the ceiling like a lifeless doll, her lacy white leotard stained blood-red. What the audience had just witnessed was the 'death' of Lady Gaga, live onstage, followed by Gaga's own not-quite-white wedding – a fittingly twisted end to any 'Bad Romance'.

Yet this wasn't the only time Gaga has raided her wardrobe to achieve a ravishing fusion of the morbid and glamorous. Her performance at LA's Museum of Contemporary Art saw her channelling the maudlin spirit of Tim Burton's Corpse Bride. Surrounded by whorls of swirling smoke and the dancers of the Bolshoi Ballet – circling her like figures in a crazed wind-up music box – Gaga lit up the stage with an emotional rendition of 'Speechless'. Inspired by Gaga's 'fear of death monster', it was the perfect soundtrack for artist Francesco Vezzoli's hauntingly beautiful show, 'The Shortest Musical You Will Never See Again'.

Gaga explained the story behind this heart-rending ballad. 'Well . . . My dad has had a heart condition for about fifteen years. I've been away and on the road and he started to fade when I was gone. So, I went to the studio and I wrote this song "Speechless" and it was about [how] my dad used to call me after he'd had a few drinks and I wouldn't know what to say . . . I was speechless and I just feared that I would lose him and that I wouldn't be there.'

On the night of 'The Shortest Musical . . .' (attended by everyone from Pierce Brosnan and Eva Mendes to the first couple of rock, Gwen Stefani and Gavin Rossdale) the pain was quite literally painted across Gaga's pretty features. Her skin was pale as fine-bone china; her lips were a perfect frosty heart (painted in a Geisha-

Left: Sweet dreams are made of this: clad in an intricate beaded gown, Frank Gehry's misty all-seeing eye atop her silver curls, Gaga treads the boards in 'The Shortest Musical You Will Never See Again'. Opposite: Back in black: behind the scenes at MOCA, Gaga's frosty eyes and delicate heart-shaped pout are reminiscent of Tim Burton's most tragically beautiful celluloid creations.

Left: Fit for a Queen: live at the Royal Variety Performance, Lady G rocks an Elizabethan ruff in cherry-red PVC, December 2009. Above: The mask is off: Gaga's tear-stained cover art for The Fame Monster.

girl pout). Beneath her right eye, you could still see the telltale tracks of makeup where crimson tears had fallen. Thanks to the mysterious spiral pattern on her dress and her glassy all-seeing eye – set in a nest of frayed, silvery leaves on Gaga's head (as per Frank Gehry's design) – it was hard to say which of Tim Burton's gothic creations she resembled most: Edward Scissorhands, Jack Skellington, or patchwork princess Sally (these last two characters get their fairytale ending in Burton's *The Nightmare Before Christmas*). In the business of fracturing fairytales – reviving the oldest tales with some pretty but petrifying new twist – few Hollywood directors can match the talented Mr Burton's dark-hearted vision. From *Edward Scissorhands* to *Corpse Bride*, each of his movies provide

fleeting glimpses of a beguiling nightmare world in which beauty and cruelty, happiness and grief are impossibly intertwined.

In an interview with *Rolling Stone*, Gaga summed up her stormy romance with heavy-metal drummer Luc Carl. 'I was his Sandy and he was my Danny and I just broke,' she lamented. And, dressed as a jilted, ghostly young bride, it seemed as though Gaga's favourite way to wear her heartache is on her sleeve like the ultimate accessory. In interview with *OK! Magazine*, Gaga revealed a little more about the writing of 'Speechless'. 'I went to the studio and played for hours, and I wrote what is going to be the greatest record of my career – a beautiful song about my father. I remember watching the mascara tears flood the ivories and I thought, "It's okay to be sad." I've been trained to love my darkness.'

And, of course, darkness and mascara tears are driving Gaga's greatest tour to date, the Monster Ball. Even before she and the Haus hit the road back in November 2009 – travelling from city to city like some beautiful, unstoppable *cirque du freak* – Gaga realised that what they'd created together was no ordinary rock show. 'I play all of my music, but it's a story,' an excited Lady G revealed on Ryan Seacrest's breakfast show. 'And the story is that me and my friends are in New York and we are going to the Monster Ball, but we get lost. Our car breaks down and we are having trouble getting there and I tell everyone, "When you go to the Monster Ball it will set you free and all of those things that you don't like about yourself won't matter anymore." And they start to lose faith in me. So, it's got a little bit of a *Wizard of Oz* inspiration behind it. And it's this really amazing sort of glam, drug-addict opera.'

> 'I remember watching the mascara tears flood the ivories and I thought, "It's okay to be sad." I've been trained to love my darkness.'

'We can't give up now. The Monster Ball is the **greatest party** on the planet!'

Ever since the tour's opening night in Montreal, Gaga's been fated to re-enact the same twisted dream for her fans, night after night. When darkness falls, she'll tread the boards once more – swirling mists catching at her ankles, the PVC crystal formations on her jade dress glinting in the spotlight, and two nervy friends huddled close by. 'We can't give up now. The Monster Ball is the greatest party on the planet!' Gaga promises them.

But seconds later, they're running scared. And it's easy to see why. Beneath the sapphire waves, Gaga is wandering blindly into danger. Soon enough blazing eyes materialise from the dark like a pair of wicked lamps . . . *all the better to see you with, Gaga.* Worse still, beneath the eyes are rows of razor-sharp teeth, protruding from between the puckered lips of the most fearful creature Gaga has never encountered. 'It's the fame monster!' cries Gaga. And, judging by the ill-tempered pout on his ugly face, he's hungry for his next meal.

'The angler fish, actually, was my childhood monster,' Gaga explained, live on *The Larry King Show.* 'My big fear was of the angler fish, so it was kind of comical to use in the show – that I'd battle my childhood fear every night before the finale.' And every night, the ending is the same. Stripped of her green tulip dress (and given her firm belief that 'you're only as strong of a woman as your fashion', this speaks volumes about her vulnerable state), she watches helplessly as the fish's tentacles wind ever closer. Of course, her fear devours her in the end.

Right: You're so jaded. Clad in pretty crystal clusters, Gaga's the belle of the Monster Ball. Opposite: Cloud nine: lacy Lady G performs at the 2010 Brit Awards.

FRACTURING THE FAIRYTAL

'YOU KNOW I'M KIND
OF LIKE TINKERBELL.
YOU KNOW HOW TINKERBELL
WILL DIE IF YOU DON'T CLAP FOR
HER? YOU WANT ME TO DIE?
SCREAM FOR ME!'

'WHEN YOU GO TO THE
MONSTER BALL IT WILL
SET YOU FREE.'

Yet it's nothing Gaga can't come back from – with a little help from her devoted monsters. 'Get out your cameras – take his picture!' she urges every single fan in attendance. 'You know I'm kind of like Tinkerbell. You know how Tinkerbell will die if you don't clap for her? You want me to die? Scream for me!' Effortlessly elfin in her asymmetric dress – with one shoulder bare and the other encased in crystals – she certainly looks like a girl who's succeeded in finding Neverland. And, as with *Peter Pan* (and, indeed, all the best fairytales), there's a moral to the story. Even with her friends beginning to lose the faith, self-belief is all Gaga truly needs to make it to the legendary party – self-belief, and a dizzying number of killer outfits, of course.

If the Monster Ball is the Emerald City at the end of this particular yellow brick road, then that makes Gaga the story's own party-obsessed Dorothy, committed to fighting her demons and killing the witch – or so *The Wizard of Oz* would have it. Yet nothing in the Monster Ball is exactly as it should be. Backstage at the Brit Awards in 2010, all eyes were on Gaga – a vision in ivory lace, rocking an immense cloud of candy-coloured hair that would have made Marie Antoinette weep from sheer wig-envy. Everyone wanted to know the muse behind Gaga's 'brand-new instrument named Emma' (the towering keytar that made its onstage debut during the Brits performance). A smile visible beneath her lacy face mask, Gaga claimed, 'She was inspired by our friend Alexander McQueen [and] made last night in heaven with magical angels!'

One glimpse of Gaga's mesmerising 'living dress' and you can almost believe it, but rather than celestial beings, this particular animatronic beauty was created by upcoming Cypriot designer Hussein Chalayan, a mere mortal living in London. What Hussein crafted for Gaga is more than just a dress; it's a technical wonder of shimmering silver fins and one giant white train, tumbling to

Opposite and above: Lighting up the night . . . with a little help from Hussein Chalayan's show-stopping 'living dress' – on her Monster Ball tour and Friday Night with Jonathan Ross, *March 2010.*

the floor in deep snowy drifts. Take a closer look and you'll realise that what you're seeing is more than just a hallucination. Unfolding like delicate dragonfly wings to reveal Gaga's face and legs, this dress is actually made to *move* – and clearly in possession of a life of its own.

With the power to transform Gaga into a shape-shifting snow queen in minutes, it's easy to see how the living dress has become a treasured addition to Gaga's spaceship-sized collection of outrageous outfits, as well as a staple look for the Monster Ball.

Journalist Caitlin Moran, for one, has never forgotten what it is to come face to face with the enchantress in her own shadowy domain. Ushered into the elegant, candle-lit chamber where Gaga likes to relax backstage, the journalist wrote: 'She *really* isn't dressed casually . . . In a silver-grey wig, she has a black lace veil wound around her face, and sits, framed, in an immense, custom-made, one-off Alexander McQueen cloak. The effect is one of having been ushered into the presence of a very powerful fairytale queen: possibly one who has recently killed Aslan, on the Stone Table.'

When Gaga tires of dressing as an angelic princess, the wicked witch comes out to play . . . literally! It's likely that Gaga's invitation to pose in the lavish December photo-shoot planned by *Vogue* magazine was more than just a lucky coincidence. 'Grace [Coddington, the magazine's creative director] has put so much time and thought into what the clothes are going to be and who the model is,' revealed Annie Leibovitz, the stellar photographer behind the Hansel and Gretel-inspired pictures. Yet, for Anna Wintour (*Vogue*'s famously formidable editor), there was only one fierce young fashionista suited to stepping into the gingerbread house in the woods, and that was Gaga. Sure enough, *Vogue*'s December Arts Issue 2009 featured Gaga as a wicked witch about to get her comeuppance, posed to the left of model Lily Cole's flame-haired Gretel, in the doorway of one monster oven.

'Gretel looks sweet enough to eat in a poufy confection,' read the caption, but next to Lady Gaga's gold jacket and frilly bloomers, the pristine Miss Cole's outfit paled in comparison. With one finger curled playfully around a lock of My Little Pony-pink hair, Gaga certainly looked wicked, and not in the Hans Christian Andersen sense of the word. When Annie complimented Gaga on her hotter-than-hell new look during the shoot, she was surely voicing the opinion of everyone on the set. 'You look good burning!' she giggled. Gaga simply replied, 'Naturally!'

Of course, not all of Gaga's evil ensembles look so divine. One particularly surreal costume change on her Monster Ball tour saw Gaga encased in a rigid glitter-bone corset – shaped exactly like a human ribcage. But to Gaga's mind, the Monster Ball is more than just an evening's entertainment. As the Lady herself stated with passionate conviction, it is 'in essence an exorcism – for my fans and for myself – where we sort of put everything out on the table and reject it. There's so much in the show about insecurity and struggle and so many of my fans are really, really, really troubled – and I was really troubled and I still am fairly

'There's so much in the show about **insecurity and struggle** – so, I guess you could say I relate to my fans in that way and I choose not to hide from it.'

troubled – so, I guess you could say I relate to my fans in that way and I choose not to hide from it. I am not interested in being a perfect, placid pop singer . . . I'm more interested in helping my fans to love who they are and helping them to reject prejudice and reject those things that they are taught from society to not like themselves – to feel like freaks.'

Whatever she's channelling on darkened stages across the globe, you can be sure it's Gaga's very

Opposite: The lion, the witch and her wardrobe: when the sun goes down, Gaga intensifies her 'fairytale queen' look with a pair of strikingly shimmery eyes.

own brand of 'ugly' – 'the deepest, darkest, sickest parts [. . .] that you're afraid to share with anyone'. Fortunately, for Gaga – and little monsters everywhere in the world – 'Bad Romance' is blind. The besotted singer of Gaga's hit single won't shy away from any of this 'ugly', simply because 'I love you *that* much'. And for Mother Monster's millions of devoted followers, the feeling is mutual.

> **'I am not interested in being a perfect, placid pop singer . . . I'm more interested in helping my fans to love who they are.'**

When Gaga opted to auction off her grisly glitter-bone corset for charity (pledging all the proceeds to the homeless of Haiti), the response was overwhelming. Inside the skeletal top, Gaga had penned a secret message, addressed to the lucky new owner of her costume. Positioned inches away from the wearer's heart, Gaga's words rendered the corset too much for any little monster to resist. For better or for worse, they wanted to know what she'd written there; proving that the truth is not always hateful – especially when it's veiled in such a deliciously darkened fairytale as Gaga has woven in the name of her fans.

Left: All wrapped up; at the Rainforest Fund's birthday extravaganza, all eyes were on Gaga's delightfully dainty white bandage dress, New York, May 2010. Opposite: Skeletal chic: from her bony bonnet down to her pearly white heels, Gaga's ensemble is perfectly matched, American Music Awards, LA, November 2009.

SPACED-OUT STYLE

'I don't dress any differently offstage than I do onstage so sometimes, I get excited and I steal my own costumes!'

Lady Gaga has always emphasised the fact that in her rigorously maintained world – of high art, high fashion, constant creativity and determined ambition – there is often very little difference between the public and the private. For Gaga, the lines that traditionally divide most performers' onstage and offstage lives are notoriously blurred. In her universe the performance and the personal can be one and the same. The fantasy of the show can be the reality of life.

'In art, as in music,' she says, 'there's a lot of truth – and then there's a lie. The artist is essentially creating his work to make this lie a truth, but he slides it in amongst all the others. The tiny little lie is the moment I live for, my moment. It's the moment that the audience falls in love.'

Gaga has taken these half truths and tiny little lies, infused them with the creativity and drive of the innumerable designers, artists, DJs, musicians, make-up artists, choreographers, dancers and directors with whom she collaborates, projected these dazzling illusions onto the world stage, and in the process created the most spectacularly deranged fusion of arena dance-pop and performance art touring the planet today.

As well as soaring renditions of Gaga's multi-million-selling songs, every night the Monster Ball offers an eye-popping catwalk show that promotes the work of the fashion industry's most cutting-edge talents, and while Gaga has made no secret of borrowing from the past, her aesthetic is equally indebted to a shimmering, spaced-out vision of the future.

Tinfoil dresses, metallic flower-petal head-pieces, disco-ball bodices, glitter-encrusted capes, diamond-dusted bodysuits, UFO-sized shoulder pads – a huge number of Gaga's outfits are straight out of a decadent science-fiction fantasy. At times she stalks the stage like a retrosexual alien queen beamed down from deep space, her rocket-powered bra ready to launch her back into the heavens at any moment, offering audiences entertainment, freedom, and perhaps even temporary salvation. 'It's just wonderful,' she enthused. 'I look out at the audience and we sing and we dance and we cry. I can't say enough about my little monsters, my beautiful fans!'

'The tiny little lie is the moment I live for, my moment. It's the moment that the audience falls in love.'

But as Gaga has demonstrated time and time again, she's just as likely to don her most show-stopping outfits in hotel lobbies, restaurants, television studios or airport departure lounges. The concerts may end, the arena lights may go up, audiences may return home, but for Gaga the show goes on – and on – regardless of the context.

'The clothing, the hair and the hats . . . when you are part of that world,' she explained, 'the public can look at my love of fashion, my love of clothing and theatre as something disingenuous, as something of a mask that I could hide behind.'

She insists, however, that this is not the case – that 'Lady Gaga' is no mere mask. She may well be able to put on and take off her costumes at her own convenience, but the persona in which she has invested so much is less easily discarded. 'What I love is the way it sets me free and the way I want my fans to be set free by it too. That was the most difficult fight for me in the beginning, and it still is a fight. It is a fight for the work every day, but I am unwavering in what I believe about my work and what I do because it is genuine. It is not disingenuous, it's not a farce, it is not artifice, it is part of who I am and it is something that I want to share with everyone.'

While fashion always comes first for Gaga, be she onstage in front of tens of thousands of fans or walking down a New York street holding a takeaway coffee, awards shows are an especially prime location for showing off some of the truly

Previous pages: Disco-ball decadence: Gaga's shoulders do the talking during a performance in New York (left), while (right) white on blonde proves a winning combination in Sydney, May 2009. Right: Sequined sorceress: Gaga conjures fashion magic onstage with We Are Plastic Ono Band, October 2010. Far right: Purple warrior: proof that leopards – albeit particularly glamorous ones – can change their spots, at the 2010 Lollapalooza Festival.

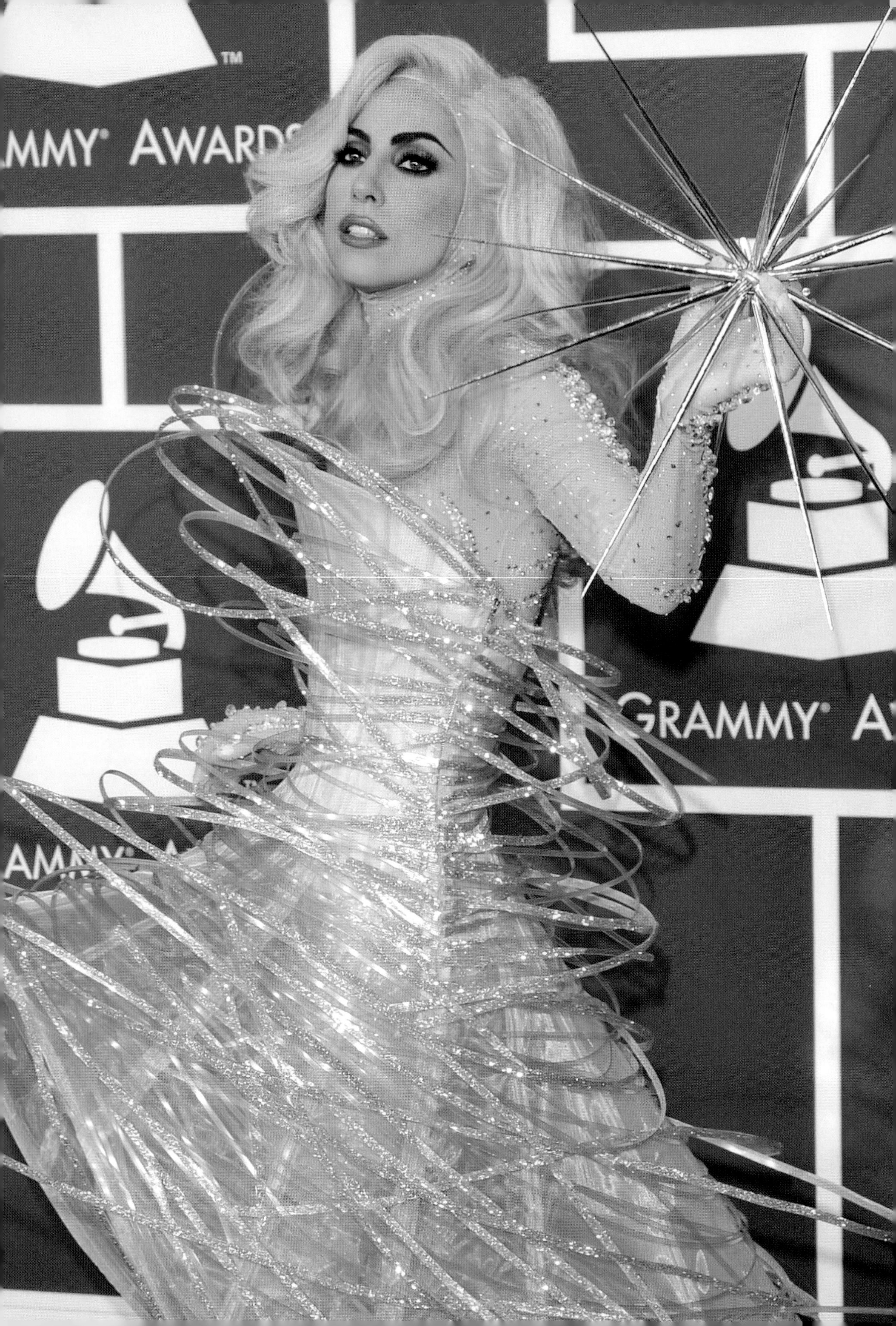
AMMY® AWARDS
GRAMMY® A

interstellar new creations she commissions. Gaga strides down the red carpet or through the ceremony or across the stage swathed in sculptural layers of glitter and sequins and diamonds and studs, ensuring that every spotlight and camera in the vicinity is aimed squarely in her direction. Nowhere was this truer than at the 2010 Grammy Awards, where she appeared in a succession of sumptuous original ensembles, all custom crafted by Giorgio Armani – though each piece looked like it could've been created in a galaxy far, far away. Armani himself released a statement detailing the pleasure he took in this particular collaboration: 'We hear Lady Gaga's music everywhere we go. It is like a soundtrack of our times. In addition to her formidable songwriting skills, she is a modern fashion phenomenon. I am delighted to be creating these outfits on such an important night for her, the Grammys, and I wish her the best of luck.'

'I can't say enough about my little monsters, my beautiful fans!'

On the red carpet, a two-tone yellow wig tumbling around her shoulders, she wore an Armani Privé purple-hued ensemble comprised of a crystal embellished cat-suit, a transparent flared skirt with a dragonfly-wing shimmer, and an endless swirl of gleaming lilac hoops that encircled the outfit like Saturn's rings. This was topped off with a spiky silver star, not unlike a gigantic Christmas bauble, that Gaga held in her left hand – an exquisite finishing touch to a dress that MTV claimed 'looked like its own planet'.

For her performance – which featured Gaga being tossed into a fiery pit during a rendition of 'Poker Face' before duetting with Elton John on 'Speechless' and 'Your Song' while playing a double-sided piano designed by Canadian artist Terence Koh, studded with black mannequin arms making the 'monster' hand sign – Gaga looked like a femme fatale superhero, clad in a legless, puff-sleeved green glitter bodysuit bolstered by towering shoulder pads, with matching platform heels and her eyes decorated with twinkling hot-pink triangles. Viewers could've been forgiven for mistaking her for an extravagantly-outfitted villainess from cult 1980 comic-book adaptation *Flash Gordon* (a high-camp intergalactic romp notorious for its abundance of outrageous Technicolor costumes). Gaga appeared to have bathed in a vat of Ziggy's own, very particular brand of Stardust.

When seated in the audience, and collecting – then posing with – her awards (she won two: Best Electronic/Dance Album for *The Fame* and Best Electronic/Dance Song for 'Poker Face'), Gaga wore a futurist jacket/mini-dress combo fashioned from dazzling white material, with jagged arm and shoulder wings, and Philip Treacy's much-discussed headpiece – which looked like either the most complex fusion of millinery and origami ever attempted by a designer, a lightning bolt, a shooting star, a falling comet, or a shard of ice, depending on who you asked. The hat was conceived by Treacy after he was shown Armani's design for the outfit it accompanied, and Gaga was vocal in her appreciation of the latter's efforts on her behalf, saying that she felt 'honoured to be wearing Armani this evening. This series of pieces Mr Armani created for me are truly iconic; they represent not only beautiful fashion, but my

Opposite: Touched by a star: this elegant space-age ensemble, created by Giorgio Armani for the 2010 Grammys, 'looked like its own planet', according to MTV.

SPACED-OUT STYLE

'The public can look at my **love of fashion,** my love of clothing and theatre as something disingenuous, as something of a **mask that I could hide behind.**'

spirit and essence as an artist. Mr Armani is a fashion legend, and tonight would not have been the same without his touch, and his wonderful team.' On that memorable night, it appeared as though Mr Armani had taken the notion of dressing a star to its very literal conclusion.

Science-fiction cinema has worked its way into Gaga's world in various ways, some obvious, some less so. Eagle-eyed bloggers were quick to point out, for example, that the ingredients listed onscreen in the blink-and-you'll-miss-it 'Cook'n'Kill' recipe Gaga uses to poison the diner's customers at the climax of the 'Telephone' video include Fex-M3 (a nerve toxin employed by bounty hunters in George Lucas's beloved sci-fi extravaganza *Star Wars*) and Meta-cyanide (a fatal venom featured in *Dune*, David Lynch's cult 1984 adaptation of Frank Herbert's bestselling science-fiction novel). The lyrics of 'Bad Romance' may name-check several of Alfred Hitchcock's classic crime films (*Psycho*, *Vertigo*, *Rear Window*), but its video's bright-white, futuristic aesthetic is pure science fiction. Two specific examples include the pods that Gaga and her backing dancers emerge from being notably reminiscent of the hyper-sleep capsules used to incubate deep-space travellers in Ridley Scott's 1979 classic *Alien*. While the lacy red-strap outfit Gaga models in the video's penultimate

Left: 'Extravagant? Moi?': Gaga adopts the intergalactic ambassadress look – courtesy of Messieurs Armani and Treacy – whilst seated in the audience at the 2010 Grammy Awards. Opposite: Tinfoil princess: Gaga performs for an A-list audience in Miami Beach, New Year's Eve 2009.

'WHAT I LOVE IS THE WAY IT SETS ME FREE AND THE WAY I WANT MY FANS TO BE SET FREE BY IT TOO.'

sequence, designed by Alex Noble, is strikingly similar to the revealing white 'bandages' outfit worn by actress Milla Jovovich in Luc Besson's visionary 1997 sci-fi fantasy *The Fifth Element*, a fashionista-friendly film whose costumes were created by Jean Paul Gaultier.

Included amongst the arsenal of instruments Gaga plays live is a pyramid-shaped keytar that resembles a weapon of interplanetary destruction or, as one *Q* journalist described it, 'a Dalek sawn in two'. (Coincidentally, a rumour – ultimately untrue – that Gaga was to make a cameo appearance in an episode of the BBC's flagship science-fiction series *Doctor Who* blazed a trail across the internet in summer 2010; Daleks being the arch nemeses of the eponymous lead character.) The glinting disco-ball helmets sported by Gaga's dancers on the Monster Ball tour, created by Alun Davies, provided another subliminal ode to sci-fi cinema, recalling the costume worn by the title character

in *Robocop* – a trashy, dystopian movie directed by Paul Verhoeven in 1987.

The pointed appearance Lady Gaga made on Oprah Winfrey's show in January 2010 was notable for a confrontational cyberpunk look straight out of director Ridley Scott's 1981 science-fiction noir *Blade Runner*. The singer wore a multi-spiked yellow hair-crown and performed – while swinging a golden mace and chain – in a black single-shouldered dress peppered with an assortment of different-sized studs and spikes, her left leg encased in a robotic studded leg brace by Brett Bailey. Olima, the Los Angeles-based designer who created the dress, explained his concept: 'I thought if Lady Gaga

SPACED-OUT STYLE

'I AM UNWAVERING IN WHAT I BELIEVE ABOUT MY WORK AND WHAT I DO BECAUSE IT IS GENUINE.'

'Being provocative is not just about getting people's attention. It's about really saying something that affects people in a real way – in a positive way.'

is doing punk, she has to do it over the top and to the extreme because punk isn't about being subtle. The dress is made from a variety of studs, not just one kind, to keep the look more authentic.' The space-age white jumpsuit decorated with hundreds of paillettes that Gaga wore while being interviewed by Oprah was designed by Nicolas Petrou. 'Being provocative is not just about getting people's attention,' Gaga told the chat-show host. 'It's about really saying something that affects people in a real way – in a *positive* way.'

Whether she's clad in a diamanté corset and wielding her disco stick like a cybernetic magician's wand to incite mass audience rave-ups, prowling the stage in a sequin-slathered leotard and lobster-claw shoes, pirouetting atop her piano clad in nothing but transparent bubbles while playing rolling fifths with her high heels, strutting out of a five-star hotel in a Jane Jetson-esque purple number, or resembling a celestial sci-fi archangel whilst wearing the dazzling 'living dress' and telling her audience, 'You make me so happy I could die,' there is little question that Gaga's spaced-out style tests the very limits of what can be achieved through fashion – onstage and in life.

Right: Victory at the VMAs: this one-shouldered couture dress by Jean Paul Gaultier effortlessly fuses the retro and futuristic. Opposite: Stickin' it to 'em: Lady G and her disco stick – a Haus of Gaga original – wow the crowds at Glastonbury Festival, June 2009.

GORE COUTURE

CNN: 'What do you say to your critics who say this is all about shock value?'
Gaga: 'Umm, you are right.'

'Is there any boundary you won't cross?' veteran broadcaster Larry King quizzed Gaga during their live television interview. But, hidden behind a pair of humungous black shades, Lady G's eyes were as unreadable as ever. 'Well, you'll have to wait Larry, I'm not sure,' she hedged, a secretive smile on her lips. 'I'm not interested in violence . . . I hate violence. I don't like negativity; I don't like prejudice. I don't believe in hatred in music.'

'I never thought I'd be asking Cher to hold my meat purse.'

Despite her occasional reticence in interviews, Gaga's work divulges all too clearly the boundaries she will and won't cross. The homicidal honey played by Gaga in the video for 'Telephone', for example, reveals a little more of what she's about: speeding away from prison in a flaming yellow 'Pussy Wagon' (driven by none other than Gaga's soul sister, Beyoncé Knowles), Lady G drawls, 'Once you kill a cow, you gotta make a burger.' Months later, it would transpire that she *really* wasn't kidding.

Fast-forward to September 2010 and Gaga's most controversial public appearance yet. It was the evening of MTV's glamorous Video Music Awards and ageless songstress Cher had just revealed the winner of the most coveted award of them all – Video of the Year. Thanks to the fabulous 'Bad Romance', it was Gaga's for the taking.

The stunning 64-year-old Cher, clad in a black mesh cat-suit decorated with sparkling rhinestone clusters, was rocking precisely the kind of risqué ensemble you'd expect from Gaga herself. But as Lady G took to the stage to collect her third trophy of the night, there was something not quite right about her glossy new gown. Rose red, velvet soft and gleaming so brightly that some viewers probably wanted to reach through the screen and touch it, the creation was beautiful enough.

So, why did Cher hang back when it came to giving Gaga her congratulatory hug? Hanging around Gaga's legs, the fringe of stringy crimson tassels looked weirdly weighty, as though cut from slabs of some impossibly glossy marble . . . Just what was Gaga's lubricated-looking dress made of?

Even without a burger in sight, it's fair to say that more than a few cows were hurt in the making of her gloriously grisly attire. 'I never thought I'd be asking Cher to hold my meat purse,' Gaga quipped as she handed over her ruby clutch bag to the *Burlesque* star. Complete with a diamanté clasp, the perfectly matched accessory did indeed look good enough to eat – after a thorough grilling at any rate! From the tip of her sirloin fascinator – blooming in Gaga's hair like a fleshy red flower – to the tips of her bloody booties, Gaga was dressed entirely in cuts of raw meat.

Previous pages: Giving 'em something to talk about – at the 2010 VMAs and as the feral face of Thierry Mugler, Paris Fashion Week, March 2011. Left: Lady in red: Gaga works her most infamous dress yet, September 2010.

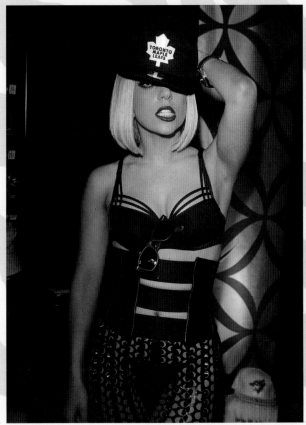

Forget the catwalk – the inspiration behind this tasty morsel came straight from the butcher's block. And, as is often the case with Lady Gaga, the result was as ravishing as it was repulsive.

Franc Fernandez, the man behind the meat (as well as the diamond headdress rocked by Gaga in the video for 'Bad Romance'), was certainly satisfied with the Lady's new look. 'The way it was cut & fitted to her body was AMAZING! Meat purse was genius!' he gushed via Twitter the next morning. 'As art piece it was astonishing! No moral judgement!' He went so far as to showcase the dress's creamy white under-corset on his personal blog. In the absence of a set of actual ribs, this was all that was holding Gaga's daring ensemble together, peeking out from beneath the sinewy material like the skeleton that should have been.

'The dress is indeed real meat from my family butcher,' the designer confirmed proudly in an interview with *MTV News*. But, though neither

Above left: Snarling darling: backstage at Toronto's MuchMusic Awards, June 2009. Above right: Hostess with the most-est: Lady Gaga gets the party started at Toronto's hottest nightspot, Ultra, June 2009.

Franc nor Gaga made any bones about the grisly origins of her super-rare frock, this is one case in which 'moral judgement' could hardly be suspended forever.

Franc's own blog was inundated with conflicting comments. For every user praising Gaga's chosen designer as a creative 'cut above the rest', there was another bent on venting their disgust. 'This is an abominable disgrace,' typed one user, clearly unable to stomach the fleshy frock. 'Could you not have gotten the same message across with artistic design using silicone or other substances to create a fake meat dress?' And, in a society where there's no shortage of vegan alternatives – whether you're shopping for go-go boots or bacon sandwiches – she certainly raises a valid question.

Hours after the event, People for the Ethical Treatment of Animals (a UK-based group of cruelty-free campaigners, otherwise known as PETA) delivered the most damning verdict of all – as voiced by founding member Ingrid Newkirk. 'In her line of business, Lady Gaga has a hard time being "over the top" and wearing a dress made from cuts of dead cows is offensive enough to elicit comment, but someone should whisper in her ear that more people are upset by butchery than are impressed by it – and that means a lot of young people will not be buying her records if she keeps it up,' she warned.

Though making a commercial killing has never been Gaga's concern – 'I don't want your money . . . I care about art,' she has protested – her devoted following of little monsters is

Opposite: Party hard . . . Gaga causes carnage at Fontainebleau Miami Beach's glitzy New Year's Eve party, 2010. Above left and right: Faking it: 'I hate fur,' fumes Lady G. Lucky for her, there's an array of cruelty-free alternatives – including fun 'n' fuzzy leopard pants and this risqué see-through cat-suit.

another matter entirely. 'I'd die for my fans,' she promised fiercely. 'And I swear to you that I'm in a place now writing music where there's this urgency to protect and take care of my fans.'

Yet the fact remains that in some people's eyes, flaunting the flesh of a dead animal live onstage seems about as tasteful as Cruella de Vil's penchant for plush Dalmatian puppies. Ingrid Newkirk went on to speculate, 'After being under the TV lights, [the meat dress] would smell like the rotting flesh that it is and likely be crawling with maggots – not too attractive, really.'

GORE COUTURE

'I'd **die for my fans.** And I swear to you that I'm in a place now writing music where there's this **urgency to protect** and take care of my fans.'

Above: Red countess: rocking a voluminous crimson cape, Gaga looks spookily sweet for her Parisian gig, December 2010. Left: Do the monster mash . . . despite her penchant for prosthetics Gaga always keeps one hand free for her beloved disco stick, live at Palais Omnisports de Paris-Bercy, France, December 2010.

Above: L is for . . . ? Featuring a hypnotic mix of swirls and spikes, Gaga's ensemble is a sanguine dream, Saturday Night Live, *October 2009.*

Winner of eight silver moon men statuettes, Gaga was in danger of losing something infinitely closer to her heart – and that's the respect of her beloved little monsters, some of whom couldn't help but wonder: In the genuinely 'Gaga' moment when she chose to don Franc's carnivorous creation, had the ordinarily humane young songstress actually been possessed? Gaga's usual attitude to killing in the name of couture would seem to suggest that yes, she had.

Back in summer 2009, pop's controversial Lady in red was still wearing green. But despite her reputation as a freakishly fabulous style queen, nothing could have prepared presenters at RTL (a popular channel on German TV) for their close encounter with Gaga that July. Wrapped in one voluminous emerald cloak, Gaga came waltzing into the studio like a crazed cartoon heroine. Glued to screens across the nation, the little monsters of Germany were temporarily

transfixed – the Lady's puffball garment was in fact made from hundreds of Kermit the Frogs. Surreally enough – peeking out above the overwhelming green heap – Mother Monster's face was the only part of her that was visible at all. Creepier still were the blacked-out eyes of the Kermits at the top of the pile, staring fixedly into empty space.

Yet, as a million stunned viewers were beginning to realise, this was more than just mindless Muppet mutilation. As Lady G herself revealed: 'The Kermit the Frog outfit is by an incredible designer by the name of Jean Charles de Castelbajac and he does a lot of museum art fashion pieces. I really loved this one in particular because I thought it was commentary on not wearing fur . . . I hate fur and I don't wear

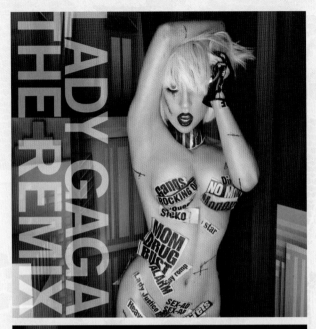

fur. We were all laughing in the Haus about how it looks like a pile of dead Kermits.'

Taking centre stage in Jim Henson's *Muppet Show*, few viewers could resist Kermit's charms – particularly not his snout-nosed crush Miss Piggy, who would have been green with envy to see her suitor on Lady Gaga's arm at the 2009 VMAs. Her date for that night was none other than the frog prince himself. 'He's been a really good date,' giggled Gaga on the red carpet. 'It's our first date, but we've been eyeing each other for a while.' And therein lies the witty statement behind Gaga's killer ensemble: If you can't stand to look into the glassy eyes of a few stitched-together puppets, how can you possibly bear to wear the genuine article?

Ironically enough, Gaga's coat of many Kermits attracted nothing but praise from inside the PETA camp: 'Genius!' proclaimed virtuous vegetarian Shawna Flavell. 'Lady Gaga has chosen a "ribbeting" way to tell the world that skins aren't in.' In the aftermath of the 2010 VMAs, however, there's not a single item in Gaga's wardrobe that's as relevant as Franc Fernandez's infamous frock tartare.

PETA and the other critics who took aim at Gaga's bloodied ball-gown appeared to overlook the fact that Lady G is hardly the first showbiz personality to swap fabric for flesh. Back in 2008, contestants on *America's Next Top Model* were made to strut their stuff clad in raw-beef bikinis, while the cover art of punk-rock band the Undertones' 1983 album *All Wrapped Up* featured a fluffy-haired mystery woman wrapped in bacon-rashers and cling-film, a string of plump sausages hanging around her neck like a gory pendant. More than two

Above: The 'body politic' gone gaga. Below: Top tips: Gaga updates the French manicure with a fun Goth twist. Opposite: 'This song is not really about loving the cameras . . .' Gaga's gore-laden rendition of 'Paparazzi' – culminating in the songstress faking her own death live onstage – was the talk of the 2009 VMAs.

'I AM NOT A
PIECE OF MEAT!'

decades before Franc Fernandez began stitching Gaga's meat dress, Canadian sculptress Jana Sterbak was ready to exhibit her own slice of edible art, 'Vanitas: Flesh Dress for an Albino Anorectic'. Cut from a staggering 50lbs of raw flank steak, the super-rare gown causes controversy wherever it's put on show. Luckily, aficionados at the Walker Arts Centre were able to see the bigger picture, realising that: '[The flesh dress] addresses issues concerning women, fashion, consumption, and the body. The equation of women with meat and the notion that "you are what you wear" are common ideas . . . In the United States, statistics have pointed to a growing number of young women with eating disorders such as bulimia and anorexia nervosa (referred to in the title), because their body types do not match the look sported by the tall, thin models populating the media.'

While Shawna Flavell may have insisted that 'skins aren't in', the quantity of luxurious leather heels, boots and handbags currently flying off shelves everywhere suggests otherwise. In today's somewhat hypocritical society, meat seems perfectly acceptable when treated in tanneries and kitchens. But wear it raw and prepare to be hunted down by the pack. However, it's arguable that prime cuts from Fernandez's family butcher could have been put to some more worthy use than Gaga's latest one-night wonder. In a world where many starving children can barely even remember the taste of beef, Lady G's fleshly gown seems a somewhat criminal waste. As the Victorian wit Oscar Wilde once wrote, 'All art is pointless.' And, to a greater or lesser extent, Gaga's meat dress is no different.

But even before Gaga and Fernandez's raw'n'ready VMAs collaboration caused such uproar, the singer's flesh-revealing tendencies were creating headlines. Cover girl for the September 2010 issue of *Vogue Hommes Japan*, she certainly didn't look out of place on

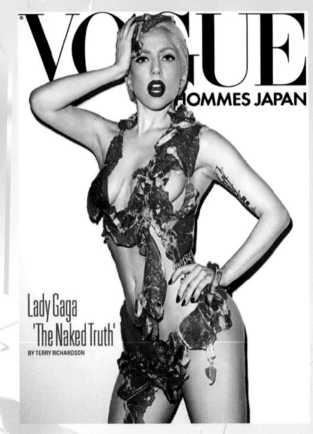

Above: Scarlet woman – Gaga's most controversial magazine cover to date. Opposite: Talk of the town: Gaga turns up the glam for her cameo appearance in Gossip Girl, November 2009.

the newsstand, blending effortlessly with the myriad scantily-clad bombshells already on display. With one hand on her milky-white hip and a perfect scarlet pout for the camera, Gaga certainly knows how to strike a pose. Yet on closer inspection, there was much about Gaga's teeny-weeny red bikini that was more sick than sexy. 'Don't get us wrong,' typed confused 'Stylite' blogger, Justin Fenner. 'Most Lady Gaga-related news thrills us, but a new photo of her has thrown us for a loop . . . We imagine PETA is going to be pretty angry about our saying this, but as gross as the image is, it's also a little fabulous.'

In fact, Gaga's 'bikini' was nothing but strategically-placed meat, strung together so as

'I CAN'T **LET MY FANS DOWN** TONIGHT, BECAUSE THEN I'M JUST ANOTHER **BITCH IN A DRESS** AT AN AWARDS SHOW.'

award,' laughs David. 'Every time Lady Gaga won, it was great. And when she won Video of the Year, I loved her meat outfit.'

'I don't like feel there are any misconceptions about me. I am whatever you perceive me to be.'

Now immortalised in the form of a carnivorous Barbie doll, Gaga was rocking her fleshy frock on behalf of Hall and his fellow campaigners as much as anyone else. When confirmed vegan Ellen grilled her on the meaning behind her raw attire – 'I get most of your outfits, but [. . .] what is the purpose of the meat?' – Gaga finally got down to the meat of the matter. 'Well, it's certainly no disrespect to anyone who's vegetarian or vegan,' she replied carefully. 'I – as you know – am the most judgement-free human being on the Earth. However, it has many interpretations, but for me, this evening, it is: If we don't stand up for our freedom, if we don't stand up for our rights, pretty soon, we are gonna have as much rights as the meat on our bones! I am not a piece of meat.'

Now she's finally found her voice, it seems Stefani will never be afraid to use it again – in defence of little monsters everywhere. In the fight against discrimination's ugliest incarnations, it's sometimes necessary to kill a few cows. But, as Gaga growls, 'People will always talk, so let's give 'em somethin' to talk about.'

Above: Out of this world: Gaga flashes her new favourite shades – Nasir Mazhar's eye-popping Alien Sunglasses – on The Tonight Show with Jay Leno, *February 2011. Opposite: Beautiful plumage: Gaga dazzles on* Friday Night with Jonathan Ross, *March 2010.*

GORE COUTURE

'PEOPLE WILL ALWAYS TALK,
SO LET'S GIVE 'EM SOMETHIN'
TO TALK ABOUT.'

GAGA ON FILM

'I feel so bad for the **"Bad Romance"** video because the **"Telephone"** video is so much better.'

I t's true that video killed the radio star, but the story doesn't end there . . .

In an era when the music video has become stagnated, imagination-starved and numb to its own potential, Lady Gaga and her Haus-mates have revolutionised the possibilities of the medium, creating videos for her songs whose twisted narratives, jaw-dropping visuals and decadent re-appropriation of pop-cultural standards have come to be recognised as major events in their own right. In late 2010 Gaga became the first artist ever to score a billion views on YouTube, proving beyond all doubt that Gaga is queen of the worldwide web.

GAGA ON FILM

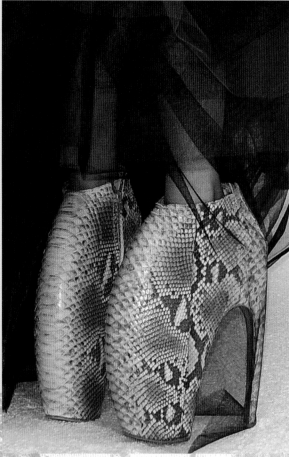

While the videos for early singles 'Just Dance', 'Beautiful, Dirty, Rich' and 'Poker Face' combined typical wasted-at-a-party set pieces with Gaga's evolving disco-trash aesthetic and an abundance of provocative dancing, the arrival of the clip for 'Paparazzi' – a hyper-stylised seven-minute soap opera fixated with sex, death and celebrity – pointed in another direction altogether. However, it wasn't until the flawlessly deranged video for worldwide smash 'Bad Romance' that Gaga's status as a pop-video revolutionary was confirmed. A high-gloss sci-fi nightmare that drew parallels between the music and sex industries whilst shamelessly fetishizing Alexander McQueen's armadillo heels and introducing a dance routine destined to be imitated in nightclubs the world over, 'Bad Romance' was as an instant classic.

The B-movie pastiche 'Telephone' – a prison-yard mini-epic awash with Gaga's kinky girl crushes, cartoon violence, mass murder and enough product placement to subsidise the advertising industry's early retirement – clocked up more than half a million online hits within twelve hours of its release and sent the blogosphere into a half-outraged, half-ecstatic frenzy. Gaga and director Jonas Åkerlund had delivered what many declared to be the most unapologetically cinematic music video since Michael Jackson's classic 1983 horror-film homage 'Thriller'.

'Alejandro', helmed by renowned fashion photographer Steven Klein and so anticipated by Gaga's little monsters that a second-by-second countdown to its premiere featured on the singer's website, explicitly courted controversy by fusing

Previous page: The eyes have it: Gaga attends a press conference ahead of her concert in Singapore, June 2009. Above left: Life through a lens: Gaga gives the assembled paparazzi a taste of their own medicine outside her London hotel in April 2009. Below left: Well heeled: Gaga showcased her love of Alexander McQueen's ten-inch armadillo heels in the 'Bad Romance' video. The ultra-rare shoes cost between $3,900 and $10,000.

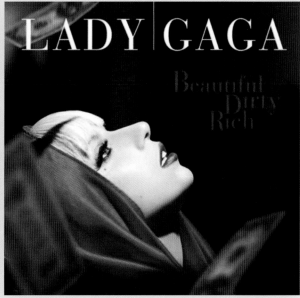

religion and raunch in a way that few other songstresses would have dared. Whatever the debt owed to Madonna's own black-and-white promo 'Vogue', certain moments in Gaga's new flick were enough to make the most controversial pop queen blush – even Madge! The end sequence in which Gaga is stripped of her red rubber nun's habit then ravished by a procession of buff backing dancers is just one example. Sporting pudding-bowl haircuts and little else, Gaga's scantily clad co-stars raised more than a few jaded eyebrows.

Gaga creates her own outfits at the same time that she writes her songs, crafting the material element of each performance to suit its musical counterpart. Her first four videos showcase some seriously desirable items – such as the glinting disco-ball bra, peeking out from beneath Gaga's top in 'Just Dance' and made by the Lady herself; the much-imitated turquoise swimsuit from 'Poker Face' that became a popular Halloween costume; the chainmail hoodie and disco stick outfit from 'LoveGame'; the Minnie Mouse-inspired hair

> ## 'All of the songs have specific outfits that go with them.'

bow featured in 'Eh Eh (Nothing Else I Can Say)' – but it was the double-whammy of 'Paparazzi' and 'Bad Romance' that proved the game-changing extent to which Gaga was capable of blurring the boundaries between fabulous fashion and infectious pop.

'All of the songs have specific outfits that go with them,' Gaga has said – and her claim makes perfect sense. Mother Monster is a girl who positively 'lives for fashion', so how could it be anything other than a core driving force behind her creative process? At least as important, if not *more* important, than the music itself. Nowhere is this more evident than in the Lady's recent videos, all of which contain uniquely sensational creations by the Haus of Gaga and the innumerable designers they collaborate with. Be it the smouldering cigarette sunglasses from 'Telephone', the spiky-headed white cat-suits featured in 'Bad Romance' or the custom-made gun bra from 'Alejandro', one thing is for certain: these are outfits and accessories that get people talking and directly impact upon the fashion world.

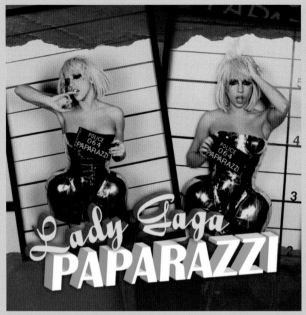

'PAPARAZZI'

The first of her videos to take viewers into the high-concept, fashion-centric Gagaverse, and to fully utilise the collective talents of the Haus of Gaga, the 'Paparazzi' promo also offers a highly literal interpretation of the song's fame-hungry lyrical content. A short-and-sweet prelude shows Lady Gaga tricked into posing for steamy paparazzi shots by her treacherous boyfriend (none other than *True Blood* hunk Alexander Skarsgård; when questioned later, Gaga confirmed, 'Alexander is a very good kisser. If I met [him] here and now I would kiss him'), who subsequently pushes her off a mansion balcony, leaving her gravely injured and – subtext! – literally destroyed by fame. The rest of the video documents her recovery, re-emergence, and revenge, as she heals her broken body through haute couture and choreography, becomes even more famous, and poisons her boyfriend in retaliation for his betrayal before confessing to the murder and being taken into police custody.

The fate of Princess Diana, who died in a high-speed car crash after being pursued through the streets of Paris by paparazzi in 1997, had a profound impact on the young Stefani Germanotta, and Lady Gaga claimed that the tragic royal was 'much of the inspiration behind the "Paparazzi" music video. When we first talked about the video, I said to Matt [Williams], "This song is not really about loving the cameras. This song is about something much more dangerous." It's about fame-whoring and seduction, but it's also about social death and Diana in truth is the most devastating and iconic martyr of fame.'

Directed by Jonas Åkerlund, a music-video veteran who has worked with artists including Madonnna, U2 and the Smashing Pumpkins, the 'Paparazzi' film introduced the now-traditional concept of the Gaga 'mini-movie', complete with credits and cast list. The production was styled by Jonas's wife, B. Åkerlund – Gaga's first official stylist, who described the singer as 'like a sister that I never had'.

- In the opening scene, Gaga wears a Thierry Mugler archive corset, with a bra by Tra La La ('because she was moving around so much and her boobs would pop out', explained B.), custom-made gloves by London designer Glovedup, one knuckle-dusting beauty of a

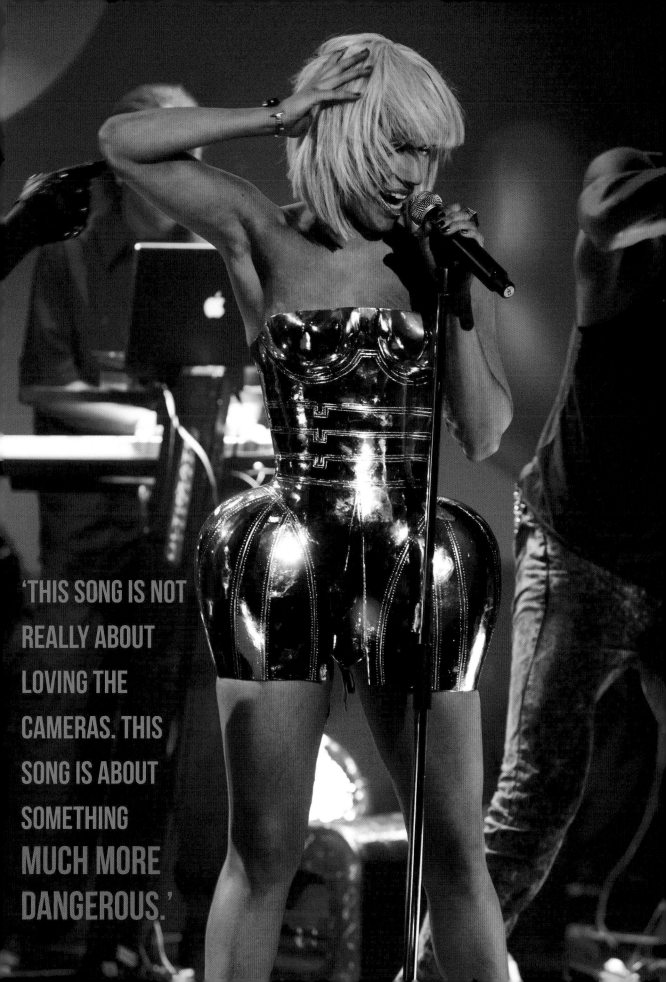

'THIS SONG IS NOT REALLY ABOUT LOVING THE CAMERAS. THIS SONG IS ABOUT SOMETHING **MUCH MORE DANGEROUS**.'

'My fascination with **death and the demise of the celebrity** goes along with me watching these **hugely iconic and amazing people** that I have heralded and admired my whole life, become destroyed.'

ring by Dior, a heart necklace by Tom Binns, diamond bracelets from Loree Rodkin and shoes by Giuseppe Zanotti.

- It's a long way down from her luxurious balcony. But even after the fall, Gaga manages to look amazing. Papped in a crumpled, bloodstained heap, her Thierry Mugler archive piece – embellished with a million shimmering crystals – is still picture perfect.

- When she emerges from the limousine, she wears a pink metal-and-crystal neck brace from Betony Vernon for Swarovski Runway Rocks with vintage shoulder pads, a metal corset from the Dolce & Gabbana archives and shoes by Balmain for Giuseppe Zanotti. The wheelchair Gaga is lowered into is adorned with Gucci fabric and embroidered with Swarovski crystals.

- The gold corset with accompanying headpiece she models when dancing on crutches is a famous Thierry Mugler 'robot' that arrived on the video's set in a padlocked box, and looks strikingly similar to an outfit featured in Fritz Lang's 1927 German expressionist film *Metropolis*.

Bow-tie beauty: Gaga struts her typically provocative stuff on the red carpet at a February 2009 nightclub showcase in Paris.

- The white body suit with layered half-skirt and a bouquet of black-and-grey shoulder ruffles is from London-based designer Boudicca, and proved so inspiring to B. Åkerlund that she made several 'low-rent' versions of it for Gaga's backing dancers at the last minute.
- On the gilt-edged sofa with not one but four of the boys from Snakes of Eden (Gaga's favourite hair-metal band), Lady G wastes no time in getting a little steamy with the blond beauties. Clad in another glossy black Mugler masterpiece, teamed with Dolce & Gabbana shoes and lightning bolt earrings, her ensemble is irresistible as the Lady herself.
- In the unsettling strobe-lit sequence, Gaga wears a vintage Mohawk headpiece and is wrapped in an outfit improvised from actual film stock.
- The yellow-and-black 'Minnie Mouse' outfit Gaga wears when poisoning her boyfriend was made especially by Jeremy Scott, and the accompanying glasses (later worn by Beyoncé when she too poisons her boyfriend in the 'Telephone' video) came from an earlier collection of his.
- During her arrest by police in her 'cone-hair' guise, Gaga wears her own vintage Emilio Pucci sunglasses, a custom-made Glovedup sparkling glove cape and a vintage bondage bra-and-chain corset made by the Blonds.
- The bauble-silver corset she poses in for her mug shot – the video's last scene – is from the Dolce & Gabbana archives, and almost didn't make it to the set because it was held up at US customs.

The 'Paparazzi' video was the first fully realised expression of Gaga's ongoing fascination with fame's dark side, and the inherently destructive nature of celebrity whenever the public persona overwhelms the individual herself. 'I suppose some of my fascination with death and the demise of the celebrity goes along with me watching these hugely iconic and amazing people that I have heralded and admired my whole life, become destroyed – whether self-destroyed or destroyed by the media.'

> 'There was this really amazing quality in "Paparazzi", where it kind of had this **pure pop music** quality but at the same time it was a **commentary on fame culture** . . .'

Gaga, to her credit, has built a chameleonic, larger-than-life mythology around herself to avoid just such a fate. She retains almost total control over her public image, inhabiting that image as an actor inhabits a character. She *is* Lady Gaga, not Stefani Germanotta, but no one knows precisely *who* Gaga is, because she is constantly changing and – if she's to be believed – never has a day off from living her own ultra-glam hybrid of truth and illusion. 'I used to walk down the street like I was a star. I want people to walk around delusional about how great they can be and then to fight so hard for it that the lie becomes the truth.'

Even during long-haul flights, Gaga is able to keep up the spellbinding charade, but she's never one particular version of herself – or, indeed, in one particular outfit – long enough for the media to pin her down. Anxious never to end up like her poisonous character in the 'Paparazzi' video, Gaga knows better than to ever stop poker facing.

GAGA ON FILM

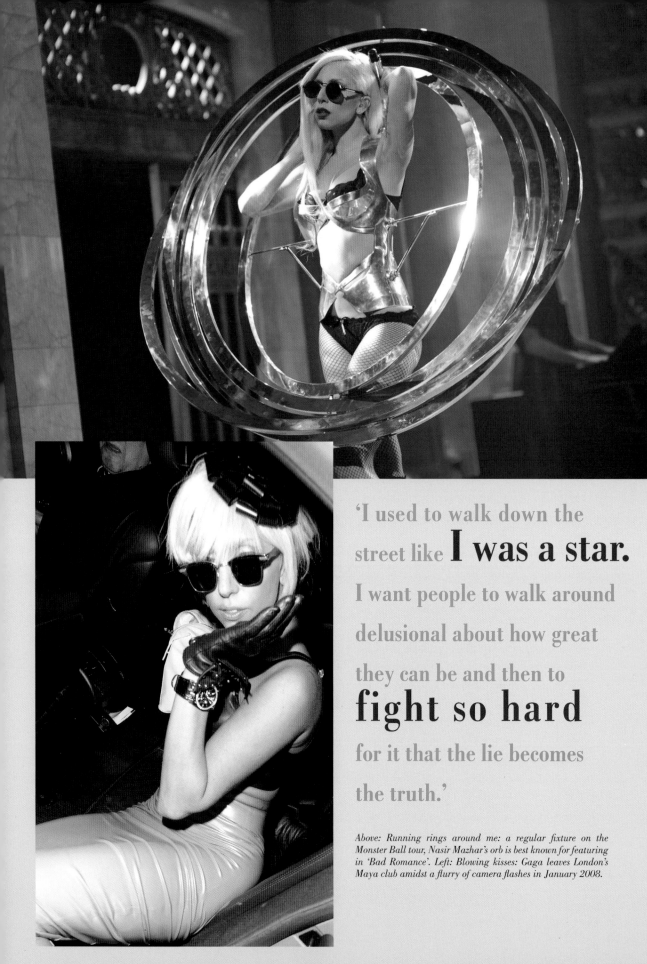

'I used to walk down the street like **I was a star.** I want people to walk around delusional about how great they can be and then to **fight so hard** for it that the lie becomes the truth.'

Above: Running rings around me: a regular fixture on the Monster Ball tour, Nasir Mazhar's orb is best known for featuring in 'Bad Romance'. Left: Blowing kisses: Gaga leaves London's Maya club amidst a flurry of camera flashes in January 2008.

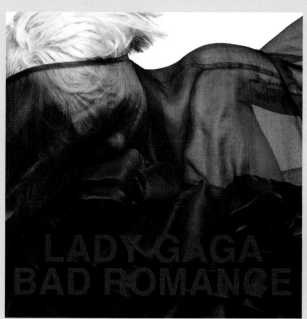

'BAD ROMANCE'

The video that changed everything, 'Bad Romance' was helmed by Francis Lawrence (director of *I Am Legend*, Will Smith's romp through a post-apocalyptic New York) and took the Haus's luxurious and wilfully warped aesthetic to the next level. Built around an infectious 'Rah-rah-ah-ah-ah' hook and a sky-sized sing-along chorus, the song is 'about being in love with your best friend'. Whatever Gaga and Lawrence created together, it needed to be a glossy evocation of the heartache that this entails. With despair, dominance and longing never far from the video's surface, they certainly didn't disappoint.

In the futuristic 'Bath Haus of Gaga', Gaga and her dancers emerge from sleek white pods, an act she likened to hatching from 'little monster eggs' – and the most powerful symbol of Lady G's artistic evolution yet. Marking a thrilling new phase in Gaga's career, 'Bad Romance' was a rebirth in more ways than one. Clad in clean white bodysuits inspired by Max's wolf costume in the film *Where the Wild Things Are* (cult director Spike Jonze's 2009 adaptation of Maurice Sendak's celebrated children's book), they rise to perform a jerky, claw-handed dance that's the perfect visual accompaniment to the song's lyrical dissections of disease, ugliness and desire.

Throughout the video, Gaga appears in a multitude of different guises, dressing as freak and fetishist, sex kitten and space alien, victim and victor: rocking some freaky anime eyes and a mass of bouncy pink curls, reclining in a bathtub wearing a semi-transparent Rachel Barrett dress; in a revealing Franc Fernandez diamond-crown outfit, forced to perform for a vodka-swilling client who proceeds to bid for her; hunched naked in a half-lit cage with a Shinji Konishi bat-hair hat, an otherworldly creature with an inhumanly protruding spine; make-up free in extreme close-up, her eyes wet with tears; frozen inside a stop-motion storm of crystals, wearing a Keko Hainswheeler mask and clutching Benjamin Cho rosary beads; dressed in the revolving metallic rings of a Nasir Mazhar orb; trailing an elaborate Benjamin Cho faux-polar-bear coat behind her before the burly Russian gangster to whom she has been sold goes up in flames and – finally – Gaga lying beside his smouldering skeleton, on the charred remains of their bed; her mascara smeared, a cigarette in her mouth, her bra spitting sparks.

Appropriately, given that Gaga premiered the song at the end of Alexander McQueen's Spring/Summer 2010 Paris Fashion Show in October 2009, the designer's work features prominently in the video. The golden, triangularly-shouldered haute couture dress Gaga wears in the opening shot is accessorised with a pair of razorblade sunglasses, designed by Gaga to represent a 'tough female spirit' (as inspired by girlfriends of hers who used to keep razorblades hidden in their mouths); the understated black polo-necked dress Gaga wears while singing in front of the mirror is McQueen; as is the puff-skirted gold-green outfit with matching armadillo heels she creeps around in towards the video's conclusion, its material shimmering under the lights like fish scales. The fantastical fairytale worlds created by McQueen for his groundbreaking runway shows were clearly a formative influence on Gaga's desire to forge her own universe – a place where the normal rules simply don't apply.

Thematically, at face value, 'Bad Romance' explores the parallels between sex work and pop stardom, metaphorically guiding the viewer through the steps one must undertake in order to 'make it' in the music industry, and illustrating the fact that – whether selling oneself to a global audience or a single client – the sacrifices and negotiations involved are, on one level at least, fundamentally the same.

'I wanted somebody with a tremendous understanding of how to make a pop video,' Gaga said of working with Francis Lawrence, 'because my biggest challenge working with directors is that I am the director and I write the treatments and I get the fashion and I decide what it's about and it's very hard to find directors that will relinquish any sort of input from the artist. But Francis and I worked together. It was collaborative. He's a really pop video director and filmmaker. He did *I Am Legend* and I'm a huge Will Smith fan, so I knew he

Left: Too cool for school: Gaga leaves Paris' exclusive 'ANDRE' restaurant in the guise of glittering governess, December 2010.

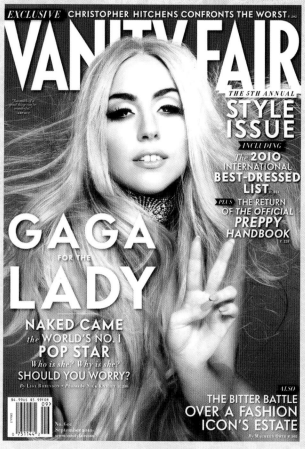

could execute the video in a way that I could give him all my weirdest, most psychotic ideas. But it would come across and be relevant to the public.'

And come across it did. The 'Bad Romance' video, like the song, was a critical and commercial smash, quickly notching up multi-million YouTube views and entering the world media's pop-culture lexicon. It received ten nominations at the 2010 MTV Video Music Awards (the most nominations for any single video since Peter Gabriel's ubiquitous 1986 hit 'Sledgehammer'), and eventually won seven categories, including Best Direction and Video of the Year. The bar had been raised to an exceptional height, and the world had one question: what would Lady Gaga do next?

Right: What's new, pussycat? Elegance meets outrageousness during Gaga's Hello Kitty-inspired photo shoot for documentary series Double Exposure, *July 2010.*

'TELEPHONE'

Conceived as a sequel to 'Paparazzi', the early scenes of 'Telephone' see Gaga's poisonous celeb get her comeuppance. Jailed for killing her boyfriend, she witnesses a fierce catfight between two inmates, but prefers to indulge in action of another kind, making out with one of her fellow jailbirds in the yard. She gets bailed out by Beyoncé, who suggestively feeds Gaga a Twinkie before the pair go on a murderous rampage, performing several bootylicious dance routines between crimes, and endorsing a seemingly endless string of commercial products – Virgin Mobile, Polaroid, Diet Coke, Miracle Whip and Wonder Bread among them. After poisoning Beyoncé's abusive boyfriend and the entire clientele of a roadside diner, they drive off into the sunset, pursued by the law, with the promise the story will 'be continued . . .'

'There is that heightened sense of your inner joy and your inner sense of self and expressing who you are.'

A mish-mashed Technicolor homage to sleaze and outrageousness, the 'Telephone' video draws inspiration from films such as *Natural Born Killers*, *Thelma and Louise*, *Faster, Pussycat! Kill Kill!* and *Pulp Fiction*, chewing up and spitting out elements of each to create a cartoonish alternate universe well suited to the song's skuzzy double-time beat and rapid fire verses, even if the onscreen action seems unrepresentative of its hard-partying lyrical content.

Revealingly, the 'Pussy Wagon' that serves as Gaga and Beyoncé's getaway vehicle was originally driven by Uma Thurman in Quentin Tarantino's ultra-violent kung-fu opus *Kill Bill*, and was lent to Gaga by the director after she explained her concept for the video to him. 'There was this really amazing quality in "Paparazzi",' Gaga later said,

Right: The long arm of the law: performing at the 2009 MuchMusic Video Awards, Gaga demonstrates that her fascination with women in a particular type of uniform predates the prison-yard chic of the 'Telephone' video.

'WHEN IT'S DONE IT **LOOKS LIKE A FAIRYTALE** THAT HAS BEEN DONE SO METICULOUSLY.'

'where it kind of had this pure pop music quality but at the same time it was a commentary on fame culture . . . I wanted to do the same thing with this video.'

'Telephone' was helmed by Jonas Åkerlund, returning to the director's chair following the success of 'Paparazzi'. He explained, 'Gaga doesn't care so much about the technical part, but she's involved in every creative aspect. We just allow ourselves to be very stupid with each other, and then you get ideas like sunglasses made of cigarettes.'

'I need fashion for my music, and I need music for my fashion.'

Like 'Bad Romance', the video was styled by Haus of Gaga creative director Nicola Formichetti. 'It was instant love,' Formichetti said of meeting his mega-famous young muse. 'I had always stayed away from celebrity and musicians before, but she was so different. Instantly we understood each other completely.'

And the feeling is clearly mutual. Gaga herself reflected, 'There is that heightened sense of your inner joy and your inner sense of self and expressing who you are – I can be the fantasy if I choose to be – that I think we share . . . When it's done it looks like a fairytale that has been done so meticulously. It's effortless with Nicola.'

This particular B-movie fairytale lasts just nine minutes. But even in this short time, Lady Gaga appears in a total of eleven different outfits, exhibiting a veritable gallery of custom-made pop-art creations, including:

- The black-and-white-striped dress with power shoulder pads Gaga wears when being led to her cell is by Jean Charles De Castelbajac.
- Gaga's infamous crime-scene tape; strategically

Above: Studlier than thou: a variation of the studded bikini created by Haus of Gaga for the 'Telephone' video gets an airing during this performance at the Staples Centre, August 2010.

placed by LA-based designer Brian Lichtenberg.

- The cyberpunk-inspired chain and jumpsuit Gaga wears in the prison yard (accessorised with smoking-hot cigarette sunglasses) are both by Amsterdam-based fashion house Viktor & Rolf.
- The studded leather jacket Gaga wears the when she's taking Beyoncé's call is by Search and Destroy. This vintage rock'n'roll look is topped off with Diet Coke-can hair rollers (an improvisational hair-curling technique Gaga credited to her mother).
- The vintage black-and-white dress with outsized hat Gaga wears when being bailed out of prison is by Thierry Mugler, the Paris-based fashion and fragrance house for whom Nicola Formichetti is creative director.
- The geometrically-shaped blue telephone

hat Gaga wears during the 'Let's Make a Sandwich' sequence is by Fred Butler, a young UK designer who specialises in one-off commissions.

- The stars-and-stripes bikini Gaga wears for the final, post-massacre party in the diner is by Haus of Gaga, while her boots are by Christian Louboutin.

- The billowing lilac and black cowboy-hat outfits Gaga and Beyoncé drape themselves in (possibly not the best choice for the quick escape they're hoping to make) are by Belgian designer Emilie Pirlot. ('One day I got an email from one of Lady Gaga's assistants asking if I wanted to make two dresses for her new video,' Pirlot revealed. 'I had to make it in one week.')

The video offers an eye-popping fashion smorgasbord, supporting Gaga's assertion that 'music and fashion always mirror each other as part of a creative context. They cannot be separate. I need fashion for my music, and I need music for my fashion.'

A sugary cocktail of pulp fiction and high art, 'Telephone' is unashamedly sensationalist, driving down the same dusty road as many all-American heroines on the run, even while refusing to make much in the way of literal sense. According to Gaga it was filmed with the intention of '[taking] a decidedly pop song, which on the surface has a quite shallow meaning and turn[ing] it into something deeper'. Whether the onscreen orgy of excess possesses that deeper meaning, or is as calorific but nutritionally devoid as the Twinkie Gaga is fed by Beyoncé, is perhaps beside the point. As pure pop spectacle, it delivers on a scale above and beyond what audiences have come to expect from most MTV-approved fare, proving that where Lady Gaga is concerned, the revolution most certainly will be televised.

'ALEJANDRO'

Directed by the artful Stephen Klein (renowned for his work with Madonna and Alexander McQueen among others) 'Alejandro' unveils a world of wintry beauty, awash with luscious imagery – gothic, religious and homoerotic – and haunted by the ghosts of Liza Minelli and Marelene Dietrich, the movie musical *Cabaret*, and Madonna's aforementioned 1990 classic, 'Vogue'.

'I had a vision and a story for the film,' director Klein told *MTV News*, 'she reacted to it, then we both collaborated . . . We shot in Los Angeles on 30 April 2010. My schedule and hers are both complicated, so it took a lot to get the days that we could both work together.'

The video depicts a long dark night of the soul in which Gaga never seems to tire of changing faces – from steampunk queen to naughty nun to 1940s Hollywood starlet to gun-wielding dominatrix. So, what's her baffling fashion transformation all about? The singer told journalist Caitlin Moran that it all pertains to the 'purity of my friendships with my gay friends and how I've been unable to find that with a straight man in my life. It's a celebration and an admiration of gay love – it confesses my envy of the courage and bravery they require to be together. In the video I'm pining for the love of my gay friends – but they just don't want me.'

Apparently, the Lady loves a man out of uniform. Filled as it is with ripped young soldiers wearing nothing more than bondage boots and high-waisted shorts, delicate male dancers tossing and turning in their beds – clad in high heels and tiny panties that look as though they were borrowed from Lady G's own collection – and a series of less than demure dance routines, the video is positively brimming with Gaga's 'admiration of gay love'.

In Gaga's beguiling winter storm, there's more than a hint of the sacrilegious, particularly in the shape of one inverted cross – stitched onto Gaga's custom-made Jaiden Rva James rubber nun outfit in the most suggestive position possible. Traditionally an anti-Christian symbol, could the offending cross possibly have been a nod to ridiculous rumours that Gaga is in fact 'a well-endowed young man'? Other visuals borrowed straight from the pages of the good book (thankfully baby Gaga was paying attention at convent school) include the snow-covered funeral procession for a heart wrapped in barbed wire and pierced with a nail – presumably representative of Jesus' Sacred Heart – and a scene in which Gaga, dressed in a red nun's habit, swallows an entire string of rosary beads.

Perhaps more so than in any of her previous clips, each new outfit represents a link in a longer chain, holding together the video's enchanting overall aesthetic – chic, dark, military, beautiful and cruel. Klein fixes his camera on a Nasir Mazhar binocular headpiece with Alexander McQueen cape that makes Gaga look like a bug-eyed industrial warrior-queen; the rose headdress by Philip Treacy with black lace Alexander McQueen dress in which she appears

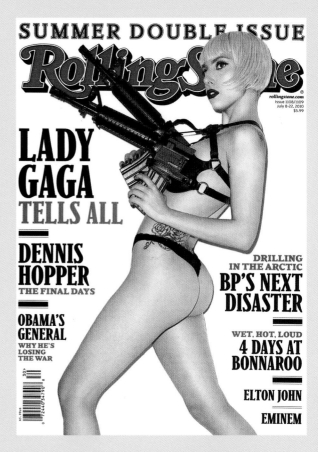

to be a widowed aristocrat in mourning; the sensual red of the nun's outfit by Atsuko Kudo that fuses snow-white virtue with burning desire; the white Calvin Klein underwear with Agent Provocateur stockings and Christian Louboutin heels that pose Gaga as a minimalistic yin to her backing dancers' militaristic yang. The simple elegance of the black Dolce & Gabbana vest with Francesco Scognamiglio pants and Pleaser heels is offset by the gun bra Gaga is glimpsed posing in seconds later (the next step up fashion's evolutionary ladder from the cone bra made famous by Madonna during the 1980s). Custom-made by David Samuel Menkes, the gun bra offers a literal depiction of how Gaga uses fashion (and sex) as armour. In her hands it's something more dangerous than your average creative outlet; it's a shield and a confidently wielded weapon.

'What a wonderful experience that was,' said Gaga of her collaboration with Klein. 'We are

'I knew his specific vision and he knew mine so that it was like tugging at a rope together … And then we tied a beautiful knot!'

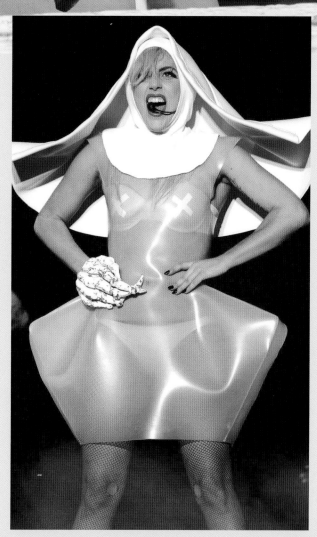

Above: Diamond vision: the bug-eyed crystal mask Gaga wore for this Today show appearance was created by leather artist Hirotake Sakai and make-up artist Chiho Omae, June 2010. Right: Back in the nun's habit: wearing a revealing Rachael Barrett dress, Gaga experiences religious devotion onstage at Madison Square Garden in February 2011.

'IN THE VIDEO I'M PINING FOR THE LOVE OF MY GAY FRIENDS — BUT THEY JUST DON'T WANT ME.'

both very strong-willed and we both have very specific visions. And I knew his specific vision and he knew mine so that it was like tugging at a rope together . . . And then we tied a beautiful knot! I wanted to bring him out of his comfort zone and he wanted to bring me out of mine. I think what made the "Alejandro" video so successful was getting Steven to look at pop choreography and my aesthetic in putting things that are really interesting, of how to sell messages and metaphors into a pop landscape so it suddenly becomes universal and means something completely different. And him stripping me down, taking off all my make-up, no eyelashes, no liner, saying "I'm cutting all of your hair off" and not tanned . . . For me, I was hyperventilating, but it did force me to be myself.'

Following the two hype-laden spectacles that preceded it, 'Alejandro' saw Gaga embracing a colder and bolder visual style. And the result? It couldn't have been further from the straightforward 'good, old Gaga times' showcased in the 'Just Dance' video. The idea of the mournful diva Gaga portrays in 'Alejandro' showing her face beneath the glittering lights of the disco ball or dancing to the boom-box beat is absolutely unthinkable. Whether the video is viewed as a celebration of gay identity, a pertinent reflection of the Catholic Church's influence on the modern world or merely a killer couture magazine spread set to music, the fact remains that Lady Gaga is changing the face of contemporary pop like no other artist on the scene.

When it premiered online, the sheer number of viewers simultaneously attempting to watch 'Alejandro' crashed Lady Gaga's website – it's an outcome that you sense would not have displeased her.

Left: Black widow: Gaga evokes a tragic glamour whilst attending the Monster Cable Party in Berlin, September 2009.

'BORN THIS WAY'

Portentous orchestra music swells, a sparkling unicorn silhouette appears within an inverted pink triangle, the camera descends through a star-flecked galaxy to observe a Shiva-like deity floating serenely in deep space, and a familiar voice intones, 'This is the manifesto of Mother Monster . . .'

So begins the video for 'Born This Way', a kaleidoscopic melting pot of surreal and startling imagery influenced by the cult science-fiction and fantasy cinema of the 1970s and '80s, whose themes include birth and motherhood, identity and prejudice, and the nature of good and evil. (Well, possibly.) Part intergalactic romp, part glitter-dusted acid trip, part slime-splattered fashionista nightmare, the video's dizzying two-minute prologue sees Mother Monster (clad in a Petra Storrs stained-glass dress, sporting a third eyeball on her chin) experience 'a birth of magnificent and magical proportions'. With Brazilian model Raquel Zimmermann acting as midwife, she creates 'a new race, a race within the race of humanity, a race which bears no prejudice, no judgement, but boundless freedom'.

GAGA ON FILM

However, Gaga's languorous voiceover informs us, this utopian race is not alone: 'Another, more terrifying birth took place: the birth of evil.' The malevolent force in question is represented by a second incarnation of Mother Monster. Perched atop a pair of thunderbolt spires and surrounded by blood-red, undulating human bodies, this dark emissary wears Thierry Mugler knife shoes and a black Sorcha O'Raghallaigh dress, and angrily wields a machine gun – one improbably produced from a risqué part of her anatomy. The reborn Lady Gaga, it seemed, had lost none of her taste for controversy.

Premiering on 28 February 2011 and racking up over four million YouTube views within two days, the video is a gaudy visual extravaganza – all mirrored split screens, oozy mannequin heads and writhing bodies – that inevitably features much limber-limbed choreography and a catwalk show's worth of decadent clothes

and accessories, with stylist Nicola Formichetti selecting pieces by designers including Alexis Bittar, Erickson Beamon, Pamela Love, Atsuko Kudo, Natacha Marro, Kobi Levi, Portolano, LaCrasia, Capezio, Billykirk and Jennifer Behr. Mother Monster's very own creation myth is, of course, impeccably fashionable.

'Born This Way' itself, a euphoric dance anthem propelled by soaring vocals and sledgehammer beats, urges listeners to love themselves regardless of their race, sexuality or the prejudices of others, and was debuted live at the 53rd Grammy Awards on 13 February 2011. Notoriously, Gaga arrived on the event's red carpet cocooned within a translucent, egg-like vessel (created by Hussein Chalayan) and carried by models. She then 'hatched' from it onstage before performing her new single in front

Above left: Corpse bride: Gaga adopts a goth-metal Miss Havisham look during a shopping trip in Milan, December 2010.

of an estimated 26.7 million viewers – offering a very literal take on the song's title, and pre-empting the hallucinatory scenes of alien labour and birth featured in its video. 'I have an idea or an idea comes and I just go with it,' Gaga told *Grazia* magazine, 'like my vessel at the Grammys. That was so perfect, the whole idea of my next album and single, "Born This Way", and then the vessel . . . or the egg as everyone kept calling it.'

Wearing facial prosthetics that appear to protrude from beneath the skin around her eyes (also featured on the 'Born This Way' artwork), Gaga – tanned and toned in Sex Trash chain underwear by Stephanie Paterek – puts her company of backing dancers through their paces before materialising in intricately painted skeleton make-up, a puff-shouldered Mugler tuxedo and

a waist-length pink wig. This look was inspired by Rick Genest, aka Zombie Boy, who stands beside her in this sequence. A model whose body and face are permanently tattooed to resemble a skeleton and skull, Genest apparently served as inspiration for the latest Thierry Mugler collection overseen by Nicola Formichetti, who identified the unconventional model as 'my muse', and also incorporated his aesthetic – akin to a permanent Halloween costume – into the Haus of Gaga's new video. (Tellingly, a remix of 'Born This Way' was used as the soundtrack for the Thierry Mugler men's show that opened Paris Fashion Week 2011, for which Gaga acted as musical director.)

'The song is very meaningful to me,' Gaga explained of the video during a radio interview, 'so I wanted to make something that would really show what was going on in my head when I wrote "Born This Way". I had an absolutely sublime time working on it. I actually did it

Above: Express yourself: this leathered Grammys look took obvious inspiration from Blonde Ambition-era Madonna. Opposite: Monster success: following Gaga's Grammys performance, 'Born This Way' spent more than a month at the top of the Billboard Hot 100 chart.

'The song is very meaningful to me, so I wanted to make something that would really show what was going on in my head when I wrote "Born This Way".'

with a UK filmmaker and a very famous fashion photographer, Nick Knight. I worked on it with him. I wrote the script for the video and concept, and between himself and Laurieann Gibson, my choreographer, we really brought the story to life.'

As well as being full of blink-and-you'll-miss-'em cinematic references (*Bladerunner*, *Legend*, *The Dark Crystal*, *Aliens*, *Superman*, *The NeverEnding Story*, *Vertigo* and *Metropolis* are some of the films directly or indirectly alluded to), the video's conclusion pays unambiguous homage to two of the most successful artists in history – Michael Jackson and Madonna. To Jackson by emulating a scene from his 1988 film *Moonwalker*, complete with white socks and gloves. To Madge by appearing in close-up with a prominent and instantly recognisable gap between her front teeth, a single tear rolling down her cheek. This was even more of a nudge-wink moment than it otherwise might have been, as when the 'Born This Way' single was first released, critics and bloggers were quick to claim that it owed more than a passing debt to Madonna's 1989 single 'Express Yourself'. Whatever the case, Lady Gaga's intentions with the first video from her third album are, in one respect at least, very clear: she won't stop until she's aligned herself with the biggest and the best. And with 'Born This Way' entering charts across the globe at number one, it looks like a goal she'll have little trouble achieving.

GAGA ON FILM

Text by Laura Coulman and Tom Branton
Copyright © 2011 by Plexus Publishing Limited
Published by Plexus Publishing Limited
25 Mallinson Road
London SW11 1BW
www.plexusbooks.com

British Library Cataloguing in Publication Data
A catalogue record for this book is available from
the British Library

ISBN: 978-0-85965-472-2

Front cover photo by Valerie Macon/ AFP/ Getty Images
Cover and book design by Coco Wake-Porter
Printed in Great Britain by Scotprint

Acknowledgements
'After all the whiskey, lipstick, and late nights editing,' tweeted
Gaga, 'the "Born This Way" video is done.' Though the making of
Strange and Beautiful was hardly so glamorous, it was a similarly
collaborative effort. And so, I'd like to extend my sincere thanks
to each of my colleagues in the (publishing) Haus of Plexus,
particularly Tom Branton (who's been a most meticulous and classy
co-author), Sandra Wake, Laura Slater and Coco Wake-Porter –
creator of the book's gloriously Gaga look, she's the gifted designer
who made Strange and Beautiful live up to its name. Thanks also
to my family – Janet, David, Pauline, Adam and Faye Coulman –
for being so very patient and supportive. The same goes for Sarah
Richards, Sarah Stubbs, Alisande Orme and Nick Pearce – all of
whom have been exposed to the 'little monster' in me during the
writing of this book!

The authors and editors would like to give special thanks to
the following newspapers, magazines, websites and television
programmes: Caitlin Moran at the Times, Rolling Stone, NY Daily
News, Kira Cochrane and Simon Hattenstone at the Guardian,
Rolling Stone, Slant magazine, the Telegraph, i-D magazine, BBC
News Magazine, Vogue US, Vogue Hommes Japan, Faces magazine,
MTV Style, Good Design, Double Exposure, Saturday Night Live,
Fuse TV, The Ellen DeGeneres Show, Wetten Daas, The Tonight Show
with Jay Leno, Friday Night with Jonathan Ross, Lisa Robinson
at Vanity Fair, It's On With Alexa Chung, the Today show, TIME
magazine, Evening Standard, Stylist magazine, Sunday Times Style,
People magazine, the Daily Mail, ladygaga.com, gagafashionland.
com, gaganews.com, gagadaily.com, ladygaganow.net, ultimate-
ladygaga.org, ladygaga.nu, dreamofgaga.com, ladygagafame.
com, worldofgaga.com, ladygagacity.com, nicolaformichetti.com,
nicolaformichetti.blogspot.com, Music Fix, ladygaganow.net,
5years.com, styleite.com, stylelist.com, charitybuzz.com, the New
Yorker, hollyscoop.com, INF Daily, Lady Starlight on MySpace,
Vainstyle.com, jc-de-castelbajac.com, armanipress.com, gaganow.
com, hardcandymusic.com.

We would also like to thank the following for supplying
photographs: Getty Images, Rex Features; Gabriel Bouys/ Getty
Images; Tim Mosenfelder/ Getty Images; John Grainger/ Newspix/
Rex Features; Scott Gries/ Getty Images; Jeff Kravitz/ FilmMagic/
Getty Images; Action Press/ Rex Features; Marco Prosch/ Getty
Images; Jakubaszek/ Getty Images; Stephen Lovekin/ Getty Images;
Sipa Press/ Rex Features; Kevin Winter/ Getty Images; V magazine;
C. Flanigan/ FilmMagic/ Getty Images; Jason Squires/ WireImage/
Getty Images; Sunday Times Style; Steve Granitz/ WireImage/
Getty Images; Florian Seefried/ Getty Images; James Devaney/
WireImage/ Getty Images; Dimitrios Kambouris/ WireImage/
Getty Images; George Pimentel/ WireImage/ Getty Images; KPA/
Zuma/ Rex Features; Greg Allen/ Rex Features; Roger Kisby/
Getty Images; Andy Sheppard/ Getty Images; Stephen Lovekin/
WireImage/ Getty Images; Steve Granitz/ WireImage/ Getty
Images; Kevin Mazur/ WireImage/ Getty Images; Tim Carrafa/
Newspix/ Rex Features/ Kevin Mazur/ WireImage/ Getty Images;
Jeff Kravitz/ FilmMagic/ Getty Images; Scott Gries/ Getty Images;
Jun Sato/ WireImage/ Getty Images; Theo Wargo/ WireImage/ Getty
Images; Valerie Macon/ AFP/ Getty Images; Michael Caulfield/
Getty Images; KPA/ Zuma/ Rex Features; Brian J. Ritchie/
Hotsauce/ Rex Features; Dave M. Bennett/ Getty Images; Copetti/
Photofab/ MCP/ Rex Features; Startraks Photo/ Rex Features; Jon
Furniss/ WireImage/ Getty Images; Rex Features; Startraks Photo/
Rex Features; Neil Mockford/ FilmMagic/ Getty Images; Jemal
Countess/ Getty Images; Jun Sato/ WireImage/ Getty Images;
Anne-Laure Fontaine/ WireImage/ Getty Images; Niki Nikolova/
FilmMagic/ Getty Images; Kevin Mazur/ WireImage/ Getty Images;
Startraks Photo/Rex Features; Michael Loccisano/ Getty Images;
Brian J. Ritchie/ Hotsauce/ Rex Features; Florian Seefried/ Getty
Images; Brian Rasic/ Rex Features; Brendan Beirne/ Rex Features;
Chris Polk/ FilmMagic/ Getty Images; NBCUPHOTOBANK/Rex
Features; Marcel Thomas/ FilmMagic/ Getty Images; Henry Lamb/
BEI /Rex Features; John Shearer/ Getty Images; Stefanie Keenan/
Getty Images; Ken McKay/ ITV/ Rex Features; Rex Features;
David Fisher/ Rex Features; Fred Dufour/ AFP/ Getty Images;
Brian J. Ritchie/ Hotsauce/ Rex Features; Florian Seefried/
WireImage/ Getty Images; Startraks Photo/ Rex Features; Kevin
Mazur/ WireImage/ Getty Images; Ella Pellegrini/ Newspix/ Rex
Features; Kevin Winter/ Getty Images; Kevin Mazur/ WireImage/
Getty Images; Jon Kopaloff/ FilmMagic/ Getty Images; Larry
Busacca/ WireImage/ GettyImages; Christopher Peterson/
FilmMagic/ Getty Images; Chelsea Lauren/ Getty Images; Rex
Features; Fred Dufour/ AFP/ Getty Images; Michael Loccisano/
Getty Images; Mark Large/ Associated Newspapers/ Rex Features;
Steve Granitz/ WireImage/ GettyImage; Francois Guillot/ AFP/
Getty Images; Jon Kopaloff/ FilmMagic/ Getty Images; George
Pimentel/ WireImage/ Getty Images; Startraks Photo/ Rex Features;
Jun Sato/ WireImage/ Getty Images; Marc Piasecki/ WireImage/
Getty Images; Sipa Press/ Rex Features; David Wolff-Patrick/
Getty Images; NBCUPHOTOBANK/Rex Features; Rex Features;
Christopher Polk/ Getty Images; c. CW Network/ Everett/ Rex
Features; Jim Smeal/ BEI/ Rex Features; NBCUPHOTOBANK/
Rex Features; Brian J. Ritchie/ Hotsauce/ Rex Features; Kevin
Mazur/ WireImage/ Getty Images; Aldrina Thirunagaran/
WireImage/ Getty Images; James Curley/Rex Features; Sipa
Press/Rex Features; Brian J. Ritchie/ Hotsauce/ Rex Features;
Sipa Press/Rex Features; NBCUPHOTOBANK/Rex Features;
Alan Chapman/ Rex Features; Marc Piasecki/ FilmMagic/ Getty
Images; NBCUPHOTOBANK/Rex Features; Canadian Press/Rex
Features; Jason Merritt/ Getty Images; Henry Lamb/ BEI/ Rex
Features; Kevin Mazur/ WireImage/ Getty Images; Anita Bugge/
WireImage/ Getty Images; Kevin Winter/ Getty Images; Olycom
SPA/Rex Features; Kevin Winter/ Getty Images.

Every effort has been made to acknowledge and trace copyright
holders and to contact original sources, and we apologise for any
unintentional errors which will be corrected in future editions.